Raising Money-Smart Kids

Raising Money-Smart Kids

HOW TO TEACH YOUR CHILDREN THE SECRETS OF EARNING, SAVING, INVESTING, AND SPENDING WISELY

RON & JUDY BLUE

THOMAS NELSON PUBLISHERS
Nashville

Copyright © 1992 by Ronald W. and Judith W. Blue

Previously published as *Money Matters for Parents and Their Kids*, 1988, Oliver-
Nelson.

Published in Nashville, Tennessee, by Thomas Nelson, Inc., Publishers, and
distributed in Canada by Lawson Falle, Ltd., Cambridge, Ontario.

Scripture quotations are from THE NEW KING JAMES VERSION. Copyright
© 1979, 1980, 1982, Thomas Nelson, Inc., Publishers.

The Scripture quotation marked NIV is taken from the HOLY BIBLE: NEW
INTERNATIONAL VERSION. Copyright © 1973, 1978, 1984 by the International Bible Society. Used by permission of Zondervan Bible Publishers.

Library of Congress Cataloging-in-Publication Data

Blue, Ron, 1942–
   [Money matters for parents and their kids]
   Raising money-smart kids / Ron & Judy Blue.
     p.   cm.
   "Previously published as Money matters for parents and their kids,
1988, Oliver-Nelson"—T.p. verso.
   ISBN 0-8407-3195-7
   1. Saving and thrift—United States. 2. Children—United States-
-Finance, Personal. 3. Child rearing—United States. I. Blue,
Judy, 1944–   . II. Title.
HQ784.S4B58 1992   91–39455
                                                  CIP

Printed in the United States of America.

ISBN 0-8407-9088-0

9 10 11 12 13 14 — 96 95

To our parents,

*who modeled financial
responsibility,*

and to our children,

*Cynthia, Denise, Karen, Tim,
and Michael,*

who daily model teachability

Contents

Acknowledgments   ix
Foreword by Gary and Norma Smalley   xi
Introduction   xiii

Part 1: The Basics

1. The Challenge   3
2. The Model   14
3. The Requirement   24
4. The Basics   37

Part 2: The System

5. The Training System   51
6. The System Continued   77

Part 3: The Results

7. An Old Time Value—Work   91
8. You Can't Have Everything   100
9. Who Is Financially Mature?   111
10. A Hated Word—*Budgeting*   120
11. Getting Money the Easy Way   131
12. Decision Making   137
13. Goal Setting   149

Part 4: Additional Helps

14. But What About . . . ?   161
15. Leaving Wealth to Children   178
16. Here's My Problem   183

About the Authors   205

Acknowledgments

We owe a deep debt of gratitude to our five children, who have taught us much about responsibility and maturity as we have watched them grow up.

Cherie Heringer has contributed enormously to the revising of this book by her comments and review of all that has been written.

Those on my staff who contributed significantly to the original publication of this material were Regina Kreiner, Kelly Nottingham, Marye Lord, and Ron Kyzer. We continue to thank them also.

Finally, for their willingness to participate with us in the writing of this book by reviewing the manuscript and writing a foreword, we would like to thank Gary and Norma Smalley.

Foreword

In our ministry with couples and families across the country, Norma and I constantly meet living reminders of an important truth. Each and every day, parents build either positive or negative patterns into their child's life—patterns that can last a lifetime.

The fact that a parent can greatly affect a child's life and destiny isn't a new discovery. Centuries ago, the prophet Jeremiah put it this way: "The parents eat sour grapes, and their children's teeth are put on edge" (Jer. 31:29).

Unfortunately, many children today have their "teeth on edge" because every time money is discussed in their home, the subject becomes sour and distasteful. Other children leave home without even the basics of financial management and stewardship, and they walk right into major problems with debt and stress as a result.

In one study alone, the major cause of divorce for couples married fourteen months or less was directly related to poor financial planning and management and the resulting stress on the marriage.

Norma and I are convinced that by reading this book and sharing its principles with your children, you'll not only be helping them learn sound, biblical principles on finance, but you'll also be helping them avoid a major destroyer of relationships.

Across the country (right next door to poor communication), inadequate money management—and its resulting stress—fractures more marriages than any other factor. And if the truth be known, many radiant brides and excited husbands enter marriage with so few financial skills that before they're halfway down the aisle, without realizing it, they could already be halfway down the road to financial and marital ruin.

That's where parents can step in years ahead of time to teach their children important lessons on finances right in their own home, instead of sending them out unprepared to learn those lessons in the "school of hard knocks."

What Ron and Judy Blue have done in this book is to provide a tremendously helpful and practical tool for parents to use with their children. Inside you'll find not only the "why's" of teaching money management skills to your children, but the "how to's" that we haven't seen in any other source.

And one more thing. Your children will not only learn practical financial skills that they can take with them, but they'll also learn the crucially important skill of making wise financial *decisions*.

You've spent years building a legacy of love with your children. The hours you spend teaching and learning with them about sound money management skills can help you protect that legacy.

GARY AND NORMA SMALLEY
Phoenix, Arizona

Introduction

While writing this book Judy and I have discussed how we were trained to manage money and how we, in turn, were trained to train our children to manage money. We realized that neither of us ever had a course in the subject or had ever been specifically taught how to manage money. No one ever told us, "This is what you are being taught." All our training about how to manage money and about how to be teachers of money management came from our own blind searching and the mistakes we have made and have learned from.

If Judy and I are typical adults, it would seem that few of us have been trained adequately to manage money, let alone trained to train our children to manage money. In doing research for this book, we looked for books on training children to manage money and found none in the Christian bookstores and only a few in the libraries. Most of those are fairly old and not relevant to today's environment. As parents we need guidance and counsel in training our children to manage their money, and we certainly know that they will not receive this training anywhere else other than in the home environment. Unfortunately many, if not most, children grow up in homes that are overburdened with debt, have no spending plan, and can be considered economic failures. So, is it any wonder that most of them grow up as economic failures?

Our objectives in writing this book are fivefold:

1. To present principles of money management.

2. To provide practical tools.

3. To answer some common questions.

4. To promote family unity and harmony.

5. To give parents encouragement.

Part 1 will deal with the basics of money management; part 2 examines the training system we use; part 3 looks at results; and part 4 offers some additional helps.

No one should think that we have *all* the answers; we certainly recognize that we don't. Like you, we are in the process, and the test will come when our children have effectively trained their children to manage money. As we observe other parents in this struggle, however, we do believe that our heavenly Father has provided us with some experiences we can pass on while they are still fresh with us.

Please prayerfully consider what we have to say before implementing it, change it to fit your unique circumstances, and pass on what you have learned to others.

The process of coauthoring a book with a spouse has great potential for creating conflict. Happily, we can report that our conflict was minimal, and we have enjoyed the process very much. That process involved doing a detailed outline together from which I (Ron) did most of the original draft and Judy edited it several times. The result is very much a joint effort.

I (Ron) would never have considered writing a book by myself on this very important subject because raising our children is a joint commitment and effort. Addition-

ally, Judy has taught me much about money management, and she has been the key player in our children's
lives in teaching them money management.

Our five children (Cynthia, 25, Denise, 23, Karen,
18, Tim, 16, and Michael, 14), as the "guinea pigs," have
played a significant role in the writing of this book, too.
More importantly, however, they are very teachable and
kind critics. They are not bashful about offering comments, and we have taken those into consideration. In
these ways they have added substantially to the book's
contents.

Part 1

The Basics

The Challenge

C hristmas in our household has traditionally been a time richly warmed with the love of five excited kids, two dogs, many relatives, close friends, and lots of fascinating surprises! These are very treasured memories. In fact, I think it's the element of surprise that often has given way to some spontaneous object lessons for all of us, increasing the wonder of our celebration of Christ's birth.

One such Christmas I gave each child a single envelope as a gift. The anticipation on their faces told of their emotions—curiosity, expectation, delight, impatience as to what was in that envelope. When they opened it, each found twenty-five dollars and a list of activities that we could do together, such as going to a professional ball game, taking a trip together, building a model together, and other things I knew each child would be interested in doing. Karen, our third daughter, decided to spend her money during a four-hour shopping spree with me.

Karen planned our shopping trip for a long time. She decided on a particular shopping center and a particular restaurant where we could have lunch together. The day finally came.

It's easy to picture a typical shopping center—rows of boutiques, department stores, card shops, pet stores— and each one wants your money. The display windows whet your shopping appetite and lure you inside to a seemingly endless inventory of goods. A shopper's delight, and a nine-year-old girl's dilemma. To rephrase a bumper sticker I've seen, "So many baubles, so little money!"

Each one of us is faced with the same dilemma every day. We have limited resources and unlimited uses for those resources.

It is possible to go all the way through high school, college, and graduate school without taking any courses in personal money management. Such courses certainly are not required in schools at any level, and very rarely are they offered as options. Should we conclude that personal money management is not very important?

Each year for the past thirty-eight years the Rand Youth Poll, a New York–based organization, has conducted a nationwide survey of teens' attitudes and buying habits. A recent survey, conducted in 1990, revealed among other things:

- "Teen-age spending practically doubled during this stretch, from 39.1 billion in 1980 to 57.4 billion in 1990."
- "Teen-agers are quick to label themselves and their contemporaries 'wasteful' in describing their shopping, spending, and saving habits. Only 17 percent considered teenagers 'thrifty.'"
- "The saving ethic, which in previous generations had been thought of as a vital aspect of money management, now appears to be largely ignored, a victim of parental neglect, inflation, materialism, indifference on the part of savings banks and the lack of adequate role models."
- "Until 1983, 'a good education or trade' . . . was considered the key to their future economic security." By 1990 the key in their minds has become "both husband and wife working."

- "Their outlays [those of thirteen- to fifteen-year-old males] are mostly discretionary and executed to fulfill generally materialistic leanings."
- Speaking about sixteen- to nineteen-year-old males who have an average weekly income of $74.25, the survey noted that "they have generally grow up in a somewhat prosperous, inflationary environment where widespread product ownership is taken for granted. They easily note the many possessions their friends and relatives have and quite naturally assume that this is the way life is supposed to be."
- Only 24 percent believe that their parents are thrifty and conservative in their buying, thereby setting an example to be followed.
- Only 30 percent of their parents urge them to conserve.
- Currently 87 percent of teenagers receive ten or more gifts per year, compared to only 75 percent in 1980.

We believe that the teen attitudes outlined above are real, but they are *not* the basic problems. The problems seem to relate to three areas:

- An uncertain economic environment.
- Lack of good role models in the family, in the church, and among national leadership.
- Poor training.

AN UNCERTAIN ECONOMIC ENVIRONMENT

Government Debt

The rapidly escalating debt of the federal government is a very significant problem. Within the last six years the total debt has increased to over $3 trillion. If you were to spend a dollar a second, it would take thirty-two years to spend the first billion dollars. A trillion is one thousand times a billion; therefore, it would take over thirty-two thousand years, spending a dollar a second, to spend $1 trillion. And because our debt is $3 trillion, it would take over ninety-six thousand years to pay back the national debt at that same rate. Even if we were going to pay back the national debt at the rate of $1 million a day, it would still take over six thousand years to pay back the $3 trillion.

These illustrations assume that we stop going into debt before we start paying it back. We presently are going into debt at the rate of over $200 billion per year. So, there is good reason for all of us to experience uncertainty. It's not surprising that so many people develop a short-term spending mentality when our own government is mortgaging our future.

Inflation

In addition to concern about the national debt, there is the fear of inflation. In the speaking that I do around the country, I have repeatedly asked those who believe that inflation is a thing of the past to raise their hands. Absolutely not one hand has gone up in any audience that I have asked, I believe, with just cause.

■ ———————————————————————————— ■

It's not surprising that so many people develop a short-term spending mentality when our own government is mortgaging our future.

■ ———————————————————————————— ■

Probably the best reason for us to fear inflation is that our government has only a limited number of options to repay the national debt. First of all, Congress can raise taxes, which is unlikely because of the political nature of our elected representatives. Second, the spending level could be reduced so that we would be operating with a surplus, but again I believe that is not politically feasible. Third, the debt could be repudiated, as it has been in other countries when inflation became an unsolvable problem, but that is not politically feasible at this time. Finally, inflation is a way out; the dollars of debt we are incurring today will be paid back with lesser value dollars in the future. To plan on, and to live with, inflation naturally fosters a short-term perspective in financial planning and decision making.

Third World Debt

Another very real factor causing economic uncertainty is the Third World debt and the amount of that debt owed to United States banks. Realistically, very few of the Third World countries can repay what they owe our banks in accordance with the terms as originally agreed. Therefore, the major banks in this country have assets that are, in effect, not worth what they are stated to be. If they were to adequately and fairly reflect the asset values at the "collectible" value (amount that the debtor nation could realistically pay them), these banks would not be able to stay in business.

Of course, these facts should cause us great fear. Without being able to do much about it at all, we live in a very uncertain economic environment.

NO ROLE MODELS

The sad truth is, Christian or non-Christian, children have very few good role models. That leaves the question "Who will teach them?" Their primary influencers are TV, teachers, neighbors, peers, church leaders, and you.

Additionally, most parents who have children below the age of twenty today are themselves no more than fifty years old. They have been raised in a period when economic times have been very good, and they have never experienced the discipline required when there are hard economic times like those their parents faced.

■ ─────────────────────────────────────── ■

The sad truth is, Christian or non-Christian, children have very few good role models.

■ ─────────────────────────────────────── ■

Peer Pressure

It is impossible to read a newspaper or magazine, watch television, listen to the radio, or go anywhere without being confronted by sophisticated and effective advertising. If you believe what you see and read, you will come to the following conclusions:

- "You owe it to yourself."
- "You deserve a break today."
- If you use this product, you will have fame, power, beauty, or wealth.
- Being able to afford it means being able to afford the payments, not necessarily the *real* cost.
- You can buy it now and enjoy it while you pay for it.
- Deny yourself nothing. If it looks, feels, smells, or sounds good to you, go for it.
- "He who dies with the most toys wins."

The daily peer pressure on both children and adults is almost unbearable. How are we to know if our neighbors can really afford that vacation, second car, new television, remodeled kitchen, new suit, or new dress? Many adults rationalize both major and minor purchases by saying, "Because we live in the same neighborhood, if *he* can afford it, I must be able to afford it too. Not only must I be able to afford it, I've *got* to have it." Children experience the same pressure, and because they, too, want what their friends have, they put pressure on parents to buy things for them.

Materialism

Adding to the uncertainty is the problem of materialism. I asked some young persons their definition of success. They indicated that they and their friends believe that being successful means "being able to have whatever you want whenever you want it." That is probably the best definition of materialism I know.

■ ─────────────────────────────── ■

"Being able to have whatever you want whenever you want it." That is probably the best definition of materialism that I know.

■ ─────────────────────────────── ■

Many people believe if they live by this philosophy, they will be able to meet all of life's needs, and they will be happy. This idea, of course, is illusory. As philosophers throughout the centuries, including Solomon in the book of Ecclesiastes, have warned, "Materialism will never bring happiness."

Judy and I took a trip to Africa several years ago with some friends. On that trip we went into the bush country in Kenya to visit with an African pastor. One of his five children played nearby with her only toy, a used flashlight battery, as we had tea outside his mud hut.

Someone in our group asked him. "What is the greatest barrier to the spread of the gospel in this part of Africa?"

His response was very insightful but astounding to each of us. I would have expected him to say something about the lack of communication, transportation, or literacy. In fact, he said, the greatest barrier to the spread of the gospel there was materialism. When we asked him to explain further, he said that if a man has one wife, he wants two wives; if he has a cow manure hut, he wants a mud hut; if he has a thatch roof, he wants a tin roof on his hut; if he has one acre of ground, he wants two acres of ground; if he has one cow, he wants two cows; and on and on.

His comments indicated to us that materialism is not indigenous to the United States. Instead materialism is indigenous to the human heart and replaces the truth with a vain and empty philosophy—one that promises much but delivers *nothing*. Materialism cannot provide true satisfaction, purpose, and accomplishment, factors that are so essential in life.

Even though we know intuitively that materialism will not satisfy our innermost desires, as families and as a nation we have developed a short-term perspective on all financial decisions, leading ultimately to our massive national and personal debts. We really believe that there are no limits on what we can spend, because if we can afford it now, the future will take care of itself. We are living blindly, ignoring the long-term consequences of the poor decisions we make.

Personal Debt

Personal debt in the United States has reached such a level that more than 80 percent of a typical family's disposable income is precommitted to the repayment of debt. The commitment on debt *must* precede using it for tithes, taxes, or living expenses, and setting aside savings for the future falls to the bottom of the list. Lenders are the only ones who have a legal priority on a family's income.

Many Americans have more debt than assets, which means that if they were to sell all their assets, they would not have enough left to pay off the debt they have accumulated. Probably very few families have ever added up what they owe and what they own, much less prepared a one-year spending plan or a budget to know whether they are living within their income. Even though they are economic failures, they don't know it. Children growing up in these homes are unintentionally being taught a way of life that almost certainly guarantees economic failure in the future.

We realize that these facts and figures don't paint a very pretty picture of our political, economic, and individual environments. But we believe that the factors we've just reviewed contribute significantly to the fear, frustrations, and conflicts which manifest themselves as family money problems—and which ultimately can tear a family apart.

OBJECTIVES

We mentioned in the Introduction that we have five objectives we want to accomplish in this book. First of all, we want to set forth some principles of money and money management that will work for families as well as children. Basic principles can apply to many different situations, and everyone can benefit from a sound understanding of them.

Second, we want to provide some practical tools that you can use in training your children to manage money. By the time they are ready to leave home, they should have specific money management skills to carry with them into their adult lives.

Third, we know you have many questions: How much allowance should you give children? Should you buy them a car? Who should finance their college education? What type of clothes should they be allowed to buy? Should they be paid for good grades? What chores should they be expected to perform? What do you do about peer pressure, credit cards, and checking accounts for children? We want to answer these questions based on our experience and what we have learned from others.

Fourth, we want to promote family unity. Over 50 percent of the persons who file for divorce in this country give a financial problem as the reason. In reality there is no such thing as a *financial* problem; it is only a symptom of a deeper problem. However, money tends to be the catalyst that leads couples to divorce, and we will address that issue in a later chapter. Additionally, much of the physical violence in marriage occurs because of money problems. Very few families make financial decisions in harmony. But family unity will be enhanced if you follow the principles outlined in this book.

Fifth, we want to give you encouragement. You *can* have harmony within a family and be able to avoid the fear, frustration, and confusion so prevalent in our society today regarding money and money management. Your family *can* achieve these goals. We hope that after you read this book, you will also be challenged: challenged to excellence in your own finances and challenged to train up your children in the way they should go (see Prov. 22:6).

CONCLUSION

The problems associated with raising money-smart kids are immense—especially in uncertain economic times. However, these problems are not yours alone. While you and your children are unique, the problems you face are, in many ways, the same ones that have been faced throughout the centuries.

The answers to these problems are not unique to this book; they are unique to what God has to say in His

Word regarding the training of children in all areas of life. We are encouraged to know that there are answers and that there is hope, and we pray that you, too, will be encouraged and have hope when you finish this book.

The Model

I n the early 1700s two men developed distinct reputations for themselves—one was Jonathan Edwards, a man of integrity, refinement, and Christian character, and the other was Max Duke, a well-known criminal. A trace of their descendants during the last two hundred years proves interesting. In Jonathan Edwards's line of descendants are 13 college presidents, 200 preachers, 60 prominent leaders, 90 physicians, 32 authors, 65 professors, and 300 farmers. On the other hand, Max Duke's descendants include 90 prostitutes, 100 criminals, 145 confirmed drunkards, 300 delinquents, and 285 who contracted various evil social diseases.

The point is as parents, we are models for our children and grandchildren, and we have a choice. We can be good models or bad models, and the type of models we are will affect future generations. Dr. Howard Hendricks of Dallas Theological Seminary has repeatedly stated that "more is caught than taught."

Where and how we spend money is largely a function of where and how our parents spent money. The same can be said for our children. We don't have to say a thing to our children to pass on to them our decisions, priorities, commitments, and habits.

After seeing behavior modeled, children will either model that behavior exactly or react to it and behave in just the opposite way.

For example, perhaps your father always bought a new car every year; chances are you will do the same. Or perhaps your parents paid cash for everything; you, as a consequence, may find it difficult to use credit cards. Perhaps your parents always ate a Sunday meal out; you may do the same. It may even be that you shop at the same stores where they have always shopped.

Where and how we spend money is largely a function of where and how our parents spent money.

On the other hand, it may be that when you were younger, you were always forced to wear second-hand clothes or clothes purchased from a discount store. As an adult, you determine that you will always buy new clothing and that your wardrobe will always represent the latest in fashion. You may have a need for recognition, for an improved self-image, or even for rebellion, and you react just the opposite from the example set for you.

Because we are models to our children, we can see four implications in all this. First, we must examine ourselves to see what we actually do model. Second, a husband and wife must have unity regarding goals, priorities, and decisions; disagreements on one or several issues can send mixed signals to children and lead to disastrous consequences. Third, a husband and wife should understand that they have well-defined roles in the marriage relationship and in the decision-making process; single parents should realize that they need to play both roles. Fourth, because training is a long-term process, we will need a plan in order to instill the principles we want for our children.

YOU NEED TO EXAMINE YOURSELF

Developing a training plan for your children starts with you. Below are some questions to help you determine if you want to pass on your personal money management principles to your own children.

1. Do you have financial goals for the next year, five years, and beyond?

2. Do you have a spending plan for the next twelve months?

3. Do you know the amount of your debt? Do you have a plan to pay off your debt?

4. What would happen to your family financially if you lost your job or income?

5. Are you tithing?

6. Do you ever spend impulsively?

7. What does your life-style communicate regarding your value system?

8. Are you saving and investing for the future?

9. Do you have a will?

10. Has your will been reviewed within the last two years?

11. Is the "breadwinner" of the family adequately insured to provide for the family in the event of his or her death?

12. Do you and your spouse ever disagree regarding money matters?

13. If someone did not know you and had a copy of your checkbook for the last ten years, what story would he write about your life?
    a) Priorities?
    b) Habits?
    c) What you read?
    d) Spiritual condition?
    e) Debt?
    f) Where you live?
    g) Other information?

Obviously these are very penetrating and perhaps even convicting questions. Although you may not have answered them all to your satisfaction, you probably now can identify some of your own problem areas. If it's any comfort to you, few people can answer every question as well as they wish.

Begin your training plan by putting your own financial house in order. Several books on the market can help you answer the questions covered here. One of them is a book I have written, *Master Your Money* (1991, Thomas Nelson).

THE NEED FOR UNITY

A young woman's husband left her when she was two months pregnant with their first child. Her husband had already been involved in several affairs, even though they had been married a relatively short time. The husband came from a home where his parents never respected the need for unity.

His father, who was a very successful pastor, was also a very strict disciplinarian, but he was absent from the home a great deal. The mother would subvert the father's authority by letting the children do whatever they wanted to do and by giving each child unlimited amounts of money, contrary to the father's desires. In turn, she would not tell the truth when confronted by her husband. The children quickly learned that they could get what they wanted from their mother, even though their father disapproved.

Through what they observed, the children learned that authority was not to be respected and that there were no real limits on behavior. The results were the children's confusion and total self-centeredness. Consequently the son had a poor sense of limits, and his behavior as an adult was consistent with the family pattern he saw modeled. He chose not to honor his commitment to marriage or to parenthood; rather, he chose to react in a self-centered way when faced with his responsibilities as a husband and father.

Disunity between a husband and a wife can have tragic consequences for the children. Dr. Hendricks has stated it so well: "Fog in the pulpit creates a cloud in the pew." Unless a husband and wife are consistent and unified in what they pass on to their children, it is only natural for the children to be confused and inconsistent.

In our own strength and energy we begin a lot of "good" things, but the perseverance to continue takes supernatural wisdom and stamina.

The commitment to unity between a husband and wife is vital. It is a commitment to communicate between themselves clearly, honestly, and openly. It is a commitment to have common goals, to reconcile differing priorities, and to define agreed-upon roles in the relationship.

We believe this commitment requires a personal relationship with Jesus Christ. Without the enabling power of God the Holy Spirit, commitments are virtually impossible to maintain over an entire lifetime. In our own strength and energy we begin a lot of "good" things, but the perseverance to continue takes supernatural wisdom and stamina.

THE NEED FOR WELL-DEFINED ROLES

Training children is a tremendous job, and God intends for both parents to perform it. Both parents, however, do not need to play the *same* roles in the training process. For example, the "earner role" (providing the income) could be played by one or both parents. The "spender role" is played by both, as well as the children. The "decision-maker role" (making significant financial decisions) needs to be played by both; the "teacher role" (dealing with head knowledge and verbal communication) could be played by one or both; and the "trainer role" (dealing with the will) will probably be played most often by the parent who spends the most time with the children, since training involves practicing behaviors until they become habitual.

■ ─────────────────────────────── ■

A plan is really nothing more than premade decisions.

■ ─────────────────────────────── ■

However the roles are divided, a decision by the parents on *what* roles each is going to play will communicate consistency, unity, and authority to the children. Consider the opposites of these three values, and you will see how important they are to success in life. Inconsistency, disunity, and lack of respect for authority are, we're sure, the characteristics that governed the descendants of Max Duke.

THE NEED FOR A TRAINING PLAN

Every day we make plans—some long-term and some short-term. Those plans can be formal or informal. The formal plans tend to focus on the more important activities of life, such as planning for retirement, college, or a new home. Less formal plans include planning for a vacation, a garden, a weekend's activities, redecorating the home, and so on.

The more formal plans tend to be more long-term and more significant, and they require you to give a great deal of forethought to them. The training of children in managing money is a very difficult and long-term task; therefore, you need some type of formal plan for that training process. It does not necessarily have to be written, but you certainly need to think it through. A plan is really nothing more than premade decisions. Then when a decision point comes up, you will have a plan from which to operate. This eliminates conflict and anxiety between you and your children. It also eliminates impulsive decisions that could be wrong.

The more formal a plan, such as blueprints for a home, the more likely there is to be clear and effective communication between the parties discussing the plan. Therefore, if you have a formal training plan, you have a tool for enhancing communication with your children. (In a later chapter we include a decision-making chart.)

Once decisions have been made and communicated effectively to children, most of the reason for conflict has disappeared. Expectations and reality become one. Conflict occurs when reality does not meet expectations. A formal plan for training, communicated to children, gives them the security of knowing where the boundaries are and what their expectations should be.

■ ── ■

Once decisions have been made and communicated effectively to children, most of the reason for conflict has disappeared.

■ ── ■

For example, if a child expects a new car at age sixteen, and the parents had never planned that, then at age sixteen the child is very likely to be disappointed, hurt, or angry, regardless of what his parents give him for his birthday. Or it may be that the child expects her parents to buy all her clothes through high school and finds out at age sixteen that the parents had no plans to buy her clothes once she was old enough to work. Again, expectations and reality do not agree and there is apt to be miscommunication, at the very least.

Communicating with children regarding their expectations will not necessarily clear up every miscommunication, but it is a major step to doing so. Not communicating realistic expectations to children gives them the freedom to expect whatever their minds can dream up, and certainly the greater the difference between the expectation and reality, the greater the disappointment, hurt, or anger.

In addition to establishing boundaries, the plan gives parents and children the track they are going to run on for many years. For example, we have communicated to our children what financial assistance they can expect from us after they are married. This is just a further extension of our money management training, yet it gives us a communication tool and the track that we, as a couple, will run on in our own financial life. Through prayer and planning, we have predetermined what our children can expect of us instead of letting them be the ones to tell us what they expect. That is what a formal training plan is all about.

SINGLE-PARENT HOMES

This is a tough road to travel financially, emotionally, and physically for any parent because there is no one to share the responsibility for the many decisions and tasks. However, there isn't the confusion with inconsistencies, miscommunication, or unresolved issues that are possible in a home with both parents. In any event, when we are talking about training, we make no distinction for those who are single parents. We are focusing on the children, and they need to learn the same skills and principles, whether they have one or two parents living at home.

■ —————————————————————————— ■

Children will "catch" far more than we will teach them.

■ —————————————————————————— ■

CONCLUSION

Mentally, emotionally, and spiritually, training children is an awesome task. Like it or not, parents are models, and whatever we model will be passed on to our children. Children will "catch" far more than we will teach them. Unless that process is bathed in prayer with much support from the Christian community, the task will be difficult at best because the world will give no support. Unfortunately, the Christian community does not always provide adequate support either.

In our experience, Christians are unsupportive not because they lack desire, but merely because they also are unsure of themselves. They do not have the answers to money management any more than anyone else and, therefore, find it difficult to support others or help themselves. It is more a matter of "the blind leading the blind" than anything else.

The commitment to train your children to be financially responsible is sobering. There's a lot of work to be done and it's a long-term job with far-reaching consequences. The principles don't end with just your children; they affect generations to come. We'll talk more about what's required in the next chapter.

We urge you to enter into this commitment prayerfully and faithfully. To help make it lasting, we suggest that you make your pledge on paper and set some initial goals. The following is an example that we hope will help.

We commit to each other and to our Lord and Savior to do the following:

1. To put *our* financial house in order.

2. To communicate, to record our goals, to reconcile our priorities, and to agree upon our differing roles.

3. To formalize a training plan by _____.

SIGNATURE   DATE

SIGNATURE   DATE

The Requirement

How long did it take you to write *Master Your Money?*" It's a question often asked of me, and my answer is always: "Twenty years." Of course, the actual writing process took only about six months, but it took twenty years of experience for me to have anything at all to say.

In examining how I gained that knowledge, I realize that most of what I learned came from the mistakes I made and my willingness to learn from them. Not only does wisdom take time to acquire, but it costs us something in terms of the mistakes we make. Training children also requires a long period of time and we make many mistakes along the way.

Proverbs 22:6 states, "Train up a child in the way he should go, / And when he is old he will not depart from it." There are two key words in this verse—*train* and *old*.

Training deals with the will, but *teaching* deals with the intellect. Teaching is included in training, but teaching is not the same as training. Children must understand what they should do; this is teaching. However, they are not trained until they, of their own free will, *choose* to do what they should do. Children can be taught to make the bed, but they haven't been trained to make the bed until they make it correctly and voluntarily, without nagging or demand that they do so. Obviously, training is a long-term process, and parents often wonder if it will ever be accomplished.

Old in this verse refers to the age of puberty. Therefore, the Scripture indicates that children will be trained by the time they reach the early teens. That means that the training process must begin early in each child's life and it must end fairly early. There is not a lot parents can do to train the will of children once they reach the early teen years. Then they have to make their own choices, and sometimes a long, painful battle between them and the Lord occurs as they make use of their ability to choose.

Children can be taught to make the bed, but they haven't been trained to make the bed until they make it correctly, voluntarily, with no nagging or demand that they do so.

Peter Lord, pastor of the Park Avenue Baptist Church in Titusville, Florida, has been quoted as saying, "A person is not discipled until God has control of his pocketbook." We would agree with this statement. Undoubtedly, this is why our Lord had so much to say about money in His parables and teaching, because money management is a reflection of spirituality.

In the book of Luke alone, Jesus uses money as an illustration in the following parables: the creditor and two debtors (7:41–43), a friend in need (11:5–14), the rich fool (16–21), the faithful and wise steward (12:42–48), the lost coin (15:8–10), the unjust steward (16:1–13), the rich man and Lazarus (16:19–31), the Pharisee and the tax collector (18:9–14), and the minas (19:11–27).

Jesus said, "You cannot serve God and mammon" (Matt. 6:24). He did not say, "You should not," or "Try hard not to," or "Be careful not to." He said that you "cannot." You will serve God, *or* you will serve money. Training up children in the way they should go means they, of their own free will, choose to use the resources God entrusts to them to accomplish God's purposes.

If we look at how Jesus trained His disciples, we can learn four principles regarding training children in all areas, including money management. The principles are these:

1. They must experience what is being taught.

2. They must have an opportunity to fail.

3. They must have feedback.

4. They must have rewards.

Mark 6:7–13 records that Jesus sent the twelve disciples out in teams of two to preach the gospel of repentance. Mark 6:30–31 states:

> Then the apostles gathered to Jesus and told Him all things, both what they had done and what they had taught. And He said to them, "Come aside by yourselves to a deserted place and rest awhile." For there were many coming and going, and they did not even have time to eat.

Jesus sent out His disciples on their own to experience what He had been teaching for them, the preaching of the gospel of repentance.

Because the disciples were on their own, they had the opportunity to fail. It is not recorded that they did fail, but undoubtedly they were not 100 percent successful in their preaching and witnessing.

Immediately upon their return to Jesus, He took them aside to hear what had happened and undoubtedly to give further instructions as to what could have been done differently. In Mark 10:28–30, Jesus assures the disciples that because they have left all and followed Him they can expect to receive rewards:

> Then Peter began to say to Him, "See, we have left all and followed You." So Jesus answered and said, "Assuredly, I say to you, there is no one who has left house or brothers or sisters or father or mother or wife or children or lands, for My sake and the gospel's, who shall not receive a hundredfold now in this time . . . and in the age to come, eternal life. But many who are first will be last, and the last first.

So we see how Jesus used the four principles in training His disciples, and these four principles can be applied in training children about money management.

EXPERIENCE WHAT IS TAUGHT

All five of our children have learned to water ski. Water skiing appears to be a fairly simple physical activity, and it is very easy to explain how you learn to get up on water skis. You merely keep your weight behind the skis and let the boat pull you out of the water. You *must* let the boat do all the work.

This may be easy to explain, but it took us hours and hours of attempts with each of the children before he or she could get up on water skis. However, after they learned to get up, the second time was easy, and the third was even easier. Very rarely did they have trouble after that first experience. Only then did it become their own. It is the same way with money management.

It is easy to tell your children that they should tithe, save, and spend wisely. But until they experience the joy of tithing, the rewards of having saved for a major purchase, and the thrill of seeing how much money they have saved by spending wisely, telling them means nothing. The training process, then, must give them an opportunity to experience what you are attempting to teach them. Only by allowing them to experience what you are telling them will it become theirs. It is at this point that training has occurred.

OPPORTUNITY TO FAIL

A young businessman was eager to learn from the founder of the company. He went to the wise old man and asked him, "Sir, could you tell me what it takes to become wise like you?"

The wise old businessman paused and said, "Certainly, my son—two words."

The young man said, "Please tell me, sir, what are those two words?"

The wise old man said, "Good decisions."

The young man thought about this and then said boldly, "Sir, can you tell me how you learn to make good decisions?"

The wise old businessman thought for a second and said, "Certainly, my son, one word—experience."

The young man said, "Please, sir, permit me one more question. How do you get experience?"

The wise old businessman said, "Son, two words—bad decisions."

This joke conveys a lot of truth. We believe you learn more from your failures than you do from your successes. We suspect that Peter was a better apostle after his denial of our Lord than he would have been had he not experienced that tremendous failure. He most certainly was more teachable and humble afterward.

Failure is a part of life. The issue is not whether children will fail, but how they will respond to failure. The best time for them to fail is while they are young, and parents are available to counsel them. (Notice we said "counsel," not "criticize.") Probably the biggest mistake parents make in training children to manage money is not giving them the freedom to fail. Parents either make decisions for them or are so critical of their decisions that children quickly learn not to risk anything on their own.

■ ─────────────────────────────────────── ■

Probably the biggest mistake parents make in training children to manage money is not giving them the freedom to fail.

■ ─────────────────────────────────────── ■

To be unable to deal with failure in any aspect of life is to be crippled. Christians, of all people, should learn to deal with failure because, in the very act of becoming Christ's followers, we have admitted our failure to live up to God's law. Children must be given an opportunity to fail so that they can learn to cope with failure and not be devastated by it. (We spend more time on this when we get into the actual mechanics of a money management system.)

FEEDBACK

While Jesus was training His disciples, it is often said of Him, "And He took them aside." He gave them explanations about what they did well and what they did wrong. His explanation or feedback was, in most cases, immediate and uncritical. Rarely did the disciples become defensive when they were taught by our Lord; and yet He was clear and direct in offering insight to them.

According to the *Nationwide Survey* of 1986 conducted by the Rand Youth Poll, 71 percent of teenagers considered themselves to be "wasteful" shoppers. If they consider themselves wasteful, I would interpret that as a cry for feedback on their decisions and behavior. If we, as parents, do not give them that help, no one else will.

When giving feedback, parents have the opportunity to point out acceptable options to children. Saying, "This is *the* only way to do it," is much less effective than saying, "This is *a* way to do it."

Most of the decisions made regarding how to spend money reflect differences in judgments and values. Many of them have nothing to do with absolutes. For example, our three daughters differ from one another in their choice of clothing, and they certainly differ from their mother in that regard. It is okay for her to give her opinion when they are shopping, but she must communicate it as an opinion reflecting her judgment and values, not as an absolute. She may not fall in love with that dress one girl just has to have; she may even think it's not a flattering choice. But that doesn't make the selection of the dress morally *wrong*.

It is imperative for you to know where to draw the line. Knowing where to draw the line comes from having predetermined what *you* want to teach your children, morally, socially, financially, and spiritually. The issue is not an absolute so far as the line is concerned, but you must know what that line is. Once the line has been determined, circumstances should not change the boundaries. Circumstances can, however, change what goes on within the boundaries. For example, you may have drawn the line at one hour of television per day. What is watched within that one hour may vary as long as the programming meets other predetermined standards, but you have not established the boundaries so rigidly that your children have no flexibility.

This is especially important when it comes to how to spend money. In this area, children need the opportunity to *make choices* within clearly established guidelines. So be careful about the feedback that you give your children in terms of something being *absolutely* right or wrong. Continue to provide feedback, however, because they have no other source that has their best interests at heart.

REWARDS

Jesus said, "In My Father's house are many mansions; if it were not so, I would have told you. I go to prepare a place for you" (John 14:2). If we, as Christians, are not motivated to obedience and commitment by that promise, we really don't understand it.

Jesus used the promise of rewards and the promise of lost rewards as a form of motivation for His disciples and, consequently, for us as believers. Rewards are biblical, they are motivational, and they provide a source of feedback.

■ ─────────────────────────────────── ■

Rewards are biblical, they are motivational, and they provide a source of feedback.

■ ─────────────────────────────────── ■

For these reasons, rewards are necessary in the training process. We have given many types of rewards to our children throughout the years. The simplest type is merely giving them a star for a particular behavior, such as cleaning their room; we have a chart on the refrigerator that is used just for this purpose. Praise, individually or in front of the rest of the family, is another type of reward, as is individual time with a parent. An occasional ice-cream cone or candy bar can also be used as a reward if the child has no health or weight problem.

Money has also been a form of reward; however, we are cautious about this because money can easily become a form of bribery. A bribe involves using money, or some other promise, to manipulate behavior for your own benefit. A reward is a promise to be received as a matter of choice by the person to whom it is offered. You may have a desire as to what you would like your children to do, but it is their choice whether they act according to the terms you set in order to receive the reward.

Our second daughter, Denise, decided to take up basketball when she was a junior in high school. That year she set a school rebounding record, but her shooting percentage was very low. The summer before her senior year I challenged her to shoot fifty shots a day. I told Denise I would give her a monetary reward at the end of the summer for the number of shots taken. This seemed to be a good way to motivate her and to teach her about the benefits of self-discipline. She completed the shots for the summer and received the reward.

During her senior year, she was second on the team in free throw percentages. During a crucial game, she was called upon to shoot a technical foul. At that point in the season, she had the highest free throw percentage on the team. Because she had worked hard and received a monetary reward for her efforts, she was able to achieve a new level of performance. She was really doubly rewarded.

On the other hand, Bruce Wilkinson, president of Walk Thru the Bible Ministries, has said, "The fear of loss of a reward is a greater motivator than the promise of a receipt of a reward." One of the training techniques we have used is giving the reward ahead of time, but taking it away if the desired behavior is not followed. For example, we were having trouble with the children being critical of one another, especially at dinnertime. After giving the matter some thought, we gave each of them a jar containing ten dollars' worth of quarters. Then we told them that for the next thirty days any time we heard a criticism we would remove a quarter from the jar of the child who made the remark, without exception. We made it clear that they could have the quarters remaining at the end of that period. It did not take more than two days for the criticism to stop.

To properly implement training, you must be committed to the process, and you must have faith. These are essential requirements.

We believe that was much more effective than if we had said, "If you don't criticize, we will give you ten dollars at the end of a month." Again, we used a reward as a motivator and a form of feedback rather than as a bribe.

PARENTAL REQUIREMENTS

To properly implement training, you must be committed to the process, and you must have faith. These are essential requirements. Without them you run all kinds of risks, and your children could be adversely affected.

You must make a commitment of time, effort, money, and self. The training process is long-term; it requires hard work; it may cost in terms of dollars; and it will certainly call for dedication of self. You should enter into this commitment prayerfully and seriously.

But commitment, which is an exercise of the will, is not enough. You need faith too. I asked a good friend of mine, who has successfully raised his children, to identify his key to that success. His response was, "James 1:5." He said that many times when he had to make a decision, exercise discipline, or give some type of feedback, he did not know what to say or do. However, God had promised him that He would provide wisdom when he asked in faith; therefore, on the basis of faith he would pray and then act, believing that God had given him the wisdom that he needed. Seeing his children, who are now adults, would lead me to believe that God is faithful to His promise because they are two of the most godly people I know.

Faith says that you are assured of the unseen. Certainly when you start the training process, the results are unseen because they are long-term. You won't know the effects your training will have on your children for many years. You must believe that God is faithful to His promise to provide the wisdom you need to train them in the way they should go.

Sadly, there is virtually no societal or church support in following biblical principles of managing money. The church doesn't provide support because the church doesn't know what to support or how to support those who try to follow the biblical principles of money management. It is more a matter of ignorance than of apathy. If the church were to take up the challenge to teach and encourage biblical principles of money management, it would become something unique in our society.

What the world has to say about money and money management is diametrically opposed to what God has to say. Peer pressure and other influences mentioned earlier will mean that for the most part you will be on a long, lonely path in training your children to responsibly and biblically handle the money that God has entrusted to them.

REWARDS FOR COMMITMENT

Is it worth it? Should you spend the time, effort, money, and dedication to train your children? Are you willing to pay the price? The answer, I believe, is found in looking at the rewards. I can think of four rewards for paying the price to live by faith and train children to be good stewards.

■ ────────────────────────────────────── ■

When you enter into this training process, you can expect to eliminate the conflict with children over money.

■ ────────────────────────────────────── ■

First of all, you can expect to stand before the Lord someday and receive the reward for what you have done. I believe that if you have trained your children to act as responsible and godly adults, you can expect to hear Him say, "Well done, good and faithful servant; you were faithful over a few things, I will make you ruler over many things. Enter into the joy of your Lord" (Matt. 25:21).

Second, you can expect them to be good stewards of the resources God has entrusted to them. You can also expect to see your children train their children to manage financial resources in a godly and responsible manner. Those of us who have trained children, and seen them go out into the world, have no greater reward than seeing them make wise decisions as they have been trained to do. Many times Judy and I say to ourselves, "What happened? How did they learn to do that?" What a thrill it is to see children making good decisions!

Third, I believe that when you enter into this training process, you can expect to eliminate the conflict with children over money. That alone is sufficient reward for many parents to make the commitment.

Fourth, you can expect to see your children, even in their preteen years, begin to make sound financial decisions. Good decisions about what clothes to wear, how to spend their extra money, tithing, saving, and planning for the future are reasonable expectations when children have been trained in the way they should go.

At no time in life are individuals more moldable than in childhood. Children desire to learn what parents would have them to learn. They are not naturally rebellious. Children rebel because of inconsistencies between what you say and what you do, between siblings, and between your reactions to similar situations. On the other hand, they are teachable, and once they experience the rewards of discipline and wisdom, they will eagerly seek to make more good decisions.

Count the costs, but the costs are nothing compared to the rewards. Your challenge is to commit by faith to pay the price to train your children in the way they should go. When they get old, they will not depart from it, and you will rejoice as you see them "walk worthy of the Lord, fully pleasing Him" (Col. 1:10).

Up to now we've talked about some pitfalls to proper money management and some challenges that you as parents face when training children in money matters. We're ready to move on to the key principles and necessary skills involved in basic money management.

Chapter

4

The Basics

Building a house is an arduous, tedious process. Before you build anything, you must first decide what you want and where you want it. Second, you have to make your plan fit into the space you can afford, which usually means that you have to compromise on something you really think you want. Third, you must lay a proper foundation on which everything else will be built. Fourth, during the building process, you must choose every fixture, wall covering, moulding, flooring, toilet tissue holder—absolutely everything your house will need to be complete. A house cannot be built without a clearly devised plan and attention to detail along the way.

Training your children to manage money is much the same process. It's not something that just happens. It requires planning, as well as understanding four basic principles and four basic skills. As we emphasized earlier, the principles are *caught*, and the skills are to be *taught*.

The four *principles* are these:

1. God owns it all.

2. There is always a trade-off between time-and-effort and money-and-rewards.

3. There is no such thing as an "independent" financial decision.

4. Delayed gratification is the key to financial maturity.

Children must see the principles lived out over a long time period. They need the chance to try, and to fail, before they know what it is that they know. On the other hand, a skill is something that is taught; once a skill is learned, it becomes a better skill through repeated practice. *Principles transcend situations; skills are applicable in specific situations.*

The four *skills* are these:

1. How to develop a one-year spending plan.

2. How to buy wisely.

3. How to make financial decisions.

4. How to set financial goals.

■ ———————————————————— ■

Principles transcend situations; skills are applicable in specific situations.

■ ———————————————————— ■

We will examine the mechanics of the money management system in Part 2 and then deal with the basic principles and skills in separate chapters in Part 3. The actual training system used may vary somewhat from family to family, but the principles and skills should not. Before we get down to specific details, however, we must start with one basic truth.

GOD OWNS IT ALL

The absolute beginning point is an understanding of the truth that God owns it all. Haggai 2:8 records God's words: "The silver is Mine, and the gold is Mine." Psalm 24:1 declares, "The earth is the LORD's, and all its fullness, / The world and those who dwell therein." In the parable of the talents, Jesus said, "For the kingdom of heaven is like a man traveling to a far country, who called his own servants and delivered *his goods* to them" (Matt. 25:14, emphasis added). Any reading of the Scriptures will lead you to the inescapable conclusion that *all* resources come from and belong to God.

How many times have you seen a hearse pulling a U-Haul? This is one of my favorite illustrations because it makes the point so well. Job said it this way, "Naked came I from my mother's womb, / And naked shall I return" (Job 1:21). We come into the world with nothing, and we will leave the world with nothing. Whatever we have to use in the interim belongs to God, whether a little or a lot.

■ ─────────────────────────────── ■

Every spending decision is a spiritual decision.

■ ─────────────────────────────── ■

Someone asked John D. Rockefeller's accountant if he knew exactly how much Mr. Rockefeller had left when he died. The accountant replied, "Certainly, to the penny. He left everything." The reality is that we are managing God's resources for some brief period of time.

This is our definition of *stewardship:* "The use of God-given resources for the accomplishment of God-given goals." The implication of this definition is that a steward is a manager, not an owner. An owner has all the rights; a steward has only responsibilities.

Probably the best illustration of the difference between an owner and a steward is the distinction between the depositor in a bank and the banker. The depositor has the "right" to do with his money what he wants, and the banker has the stewardship responsibility of handling these resources because they belong to the depositor, not to the banker himself.

Truly believing that God owns it all has three implications. First, He can take whatever He wants whenever He wants. Second, every spending decision is a spiritual decision. Third, stewardship cannot be faked.

God Can Take What He Wants

If God can take whatever He wants whenever He wants, you should hold all resources with an open hand. God puts into your hand whatever He chooses to entrust you with, and He has the right to take out of that hand whatever He desires. When He takes anything out, you, as a steward and manager of His resources, should feel no regrets because those resources belong to Him. You should heed the wisdom of these words: "The LORD gave, and the LORD has taken away; / Blessed be the name of the LORD" (Job 1:21).

We have been asked, "How much is enough?" many times; and we believe that it relates to the openhand principle. When you close your hand and say, "God, You no longer have the right to take Your resources," you have crossed the line from *stewardship* (responsibilities) into *ownership* (rights). Only God is the true owner.

If your heart attitude is one that believes God can take whatever He wants whenever He wants it, your fear of economic uncertainty is removed. If there is an economic collapse of some sort and God destroys the economic system, you can cope because you recognize that the resources are God's and He is choosing to use them in a different way.

People who hold the ownership rights of their resources have great fear of an economic disaster. It could be a personal disaster, with all personal assets lost, or a national economic collapse, which affects everyone in the country. In either case, those who "own" their lives, children, and possessions will be devastated. True stewards may be shaken, but not destroyed, because they know God is at work.

Additionally, believing that God can take whatever He wants whenever He wants will give your decision making its proper perspective. You will make your decisions as a steward. Knowing they are God's resources will give you a long-term perspective in decision making and cause you to use spiritual priorities in making financial decisions. The question to ask yourself is this: How does God want me to use these resources? Considering this question will remind you that you are not managing your own resources.

Spending Decisions Equal Spiritual Decisions

The second implication of believing that God owns it all is that every spending decision is a spiritual decision. In other words, there is nothing more spiritual about tithing than paying for a vacation. Why? Because tithing is the use of God's resources to accomplish God's purposes. We are not saying, "Don't tithe." Just consider what is the *real* goal of God's plans and purposes for your life and the lives of your family members. It may be to build family unity, and a vacation is a way to build that unity.

There is nothing more spiritual about tithing than paying for a vacation.

Money is nothing more than one of the resources God uses to accomplish the real goals and objectives of life! For example, one real goal is security. But the only real security is through a personal relationship with Jesus Christ. Money cannot buy this, and any attempt to use money to buy security will ultimately fail. God will allow it to fail, so you must trust Him for your security both now and for all eternity. God wants you to be secure in Him.

Believing that every spending decision is a spiritual decision can have three results. The first one is the *freedom* that comes from knowing God has an ultimate plan for your life and has given you the financial resources to accomplish that plan. You are freed from the guilt of wondering whether you are spending His resources properly. This is the most exciting result and certainly a positive one.

The other two results are negative because, as human beings, we become legalistic, always wanting a set of rules to live by, and forget that we "stand fast . . . in the liberty by which Christ has made us free" (Gal. 5:1) and that God "gives us richly all things to enjoy" (1 Tim. 6:17). These are the two results to guard against.

One of them is *guilt*, which is most apt to occur when you know that you are spending God's resources on "selfish" pursuits. You need to realize you have made a willful decision when you use His resources to accomplish your purposes and plans rather than His purposes and plans. When you step back and once again realize they are God's resources, you can be free to obey what God wants you to do with them.

Such lack of obedience reminds me of our black lab, Maggie. At a year old, Maggie is a seventy-pound bundle of exuberance. Her most endearing characteristic is that she very obviously and desperately wants to please. When you pet her and give her attention, she is the most affectionate animal that there could be. However, periodically Maggie blows it. It's usually in the form of chewing up something that she knows she shouldn't or digging a hole where we did not plan to have one. When confronted with her disobedience, her ears droop and her eyes take on a very sad look. She is obviously repentant and guilty for doing what she knows is wrong. I think when we pursue our own selfish interests in money management, or anything else for that matter, we experience feelings of guilt. We are not entirely satisfied again until, like Maggie, we are back in favor with our Master, who in this case is our Lord.

People who are afraid to make a decision—because of the fear of making a mistake with God's resources—are forever in financial bondage.

The other negative result can be *rigidity*. People who are afraid to make a decision—because of the fear of making a mistake with God's resources—are forever in financial bondage. This bondage occurs regardless of the amount of resources entrusted to them.

At a conference recently I was approached by a very shabbily dressed woman. As she talked, I realized that this woman, who appeared to be poverty-stricken, was actually very wealthy. I was shocked as she rattled off large sums of money she had stashed in savings accounts, investments, real estate, and prepayments on a retirement home. Her concern was where to invest money in order to have total security. This woman was fearful of making a financial mistake that she couldn't experience the freedom of using the resources that God had entrusted to her. Christ has truly made us free, and yet she experienced anything but freedom. (Gal. 5:1).

Think of the freedom that comes from knowing that God has given you resources to manage and that He has given you guidelines on how to manage them to accomplish the real goals and objectives of life. You are not left alone to make spending decisions. God has given you His Word, a sound mind, and the wisdom to use His resources properly.

Stewardship Cannot Be Faked

The third implication of believing that God owns it all is that stewardship cannot be faked. Your checkbook tells how you chose to use God's resources. Your checkbook reveals the priorities in your life. It reveals facts such as how you manage your time, what size family you have, where you live, how much debt you have, how much you are allocating to savings and investments, how you dress, and so on.

Every other area, except the financial one, of the Christian life can be faked. A person need only be a Christian for a short time to know how to pray, how to witness, where to go to church, or how to study the Bible. These can be done without revealing the person's real motive.

■ ────────────────────────── ■

Your checkbook reveals the priorities of your life.

■ ────────────────────────── ■

However, the checkbook reveals one's actual commitment to the use of God's resources to accomplish God's purposes. I sometimes wonder if, when we get to heaven, all our check registers will have preceded us. If so, then we can spend time in eternity reviewing how we used or abused His resources.

HOW TO TRAIN YOUR CHILDREN THAT GOD OWNS IT ALL

To train your children that God owns it all, you must begin by modeling that attitude. Model prayerful financial decision making. Model an attitude that says, "I am responsible to handle God's resources because they do not belong to me, and He has all the rights." Show your children that you control financial resources instead of being controlled by them. In other words, illustrate your own freedom in the area of money and money management.

Probably the most significant way to model the truth that God owns it all is in the area of tithing and giving. Anyone who truly believes that God owns it all will freely give, with the tithe being merely the beginning point of giving.

One way to do this is to have family times when giving decisions are made. Periodically, we sit down with our children and evaluate the requests for funds that we have received. We make decisions about particular needs and how much to give to each one. We have found that in most cases our children are much more likely to give, even out of their own resources, than we are.

One summer our family received numerous requests from high school and college students to support their summer ministry. My first inclination was to decline them all, mostly out of frustration more than anything else. But as a family, we discussed the requests over dinner and decided that we would give money to each one of the requests. We communicated to our children the importance of spreading the good news of Jesus Christ, as well as allowed them to participate in the giving decision. Because of their influence, we ended up supporting all of the students that summer and contributing greatly to a variety of ministries.

In chapter 5 we will explain the money management system we use. One key point is that our children are required to tithe from their allowances and gift moneys. In this way they learn that God does own it all and that the tithe is a recognition of God's ownership, not a return to Him of "His share."

Do you reflect an attitude of stewardship with all that you possess? The best test is to think about how you treat the financial resources and all the other resources—home, clothes, cars, time, and so on—God has entrusted to you. Do you communicate a willingness to give on a regular basis, to give at special times, and to give when a need is known?

Our challenge to you is fourfold. First, if you have never done so, commit to the Lord to give up the ownership of His resources. That ownership may be in the area of money, but it also may be your home, time, or other resources God has entrusted to you. Prayerfully return those resources to Him just as if He were a "depositor" in your bank, you were the banker, and He asked to see His resources.

Second, in obedience to the Scriptures, give regularly as God has prospered you. First Corinthians 16:2 says, "On the first day of the week let each one of you lay something aside, storing up as he may prosper, that there be no collections when I come." This will communicate more than words the truth that you believe God owns it all, and your children, in turn, will catch that truth.

Third, as you are confronted with the needs of the poor, the homeless, the missionaries, the church, and so on, play some part in meeting those needs. Remember, that may be the very reason God has entrusted some of His resources to you. You are to be a channel to meet the needs of others.

Fourth, when your children are very young, require

them to tithe so that tithing and giving become habitual. If that is done on a weekly basis, fifty-two times a year, they must, subconsciously at least, recognized that they are returning to God a portion of what He has entrusted to them.

■ ──────────────────────────── ■

Believing that God owns it all will give you total freedom from financial bondage.

■ ──────────────────────────── ■

Believing that God owns it all will give you, and subsequently your children, total freedom from financial bondage. With an understanding of this most important basic principle, you can now implement with your child a system that puts all we've discussed so far into action.

Part 2

The System

The Training System

We learn so much from those who have gone before us. For instance, probably the simplest yet most effective approach to managing money can be found in Grandma's cookie jar. That's right! This method is nothing more that putting income received into the jar and taking money out of the jar as needs arise. When the jar is empty, that signals the end of spending. There are no credit advances.

This method demonstrates a basic, but profound, financial planning principle. The cookie jar is not a bottomless pit; therefore, the outgo can never be greater than the inflow. There is no such thing as a credit card or debt. With this method it is not possible to overextend yourself financially.

An alternative to the cookie jar method of budgeting is to use more than one cookie jar. In training our children, we have used multiple "cookie jars," which are merely stationery-sized envelopes with a label on the outside indicating how the cash in the envelope is to be used. These envelopes are kept in a simple file box or recipe box.

The same principles apply for the envelopes as for the cookie jar. The envelope is not a bottomless pit, and the spending can never be greater than the amount originally put in.

Two elements are necessary in any budget, be it a family budget, a business budget, or a government budget. Those elements are a *plan* for spending and a system of *controls* to ensure that the spending is never greater than the plan has indicated. Absolutely every budget must work under these two elements; and the envelope system and the cookie jar system include these elements in their most basic forms.

■ ——————————————————————————————— ■

Credit allows us to live in the short term, as if there were no bottom to the cookie jar and, therefore, no limit to our spending.

■ ——————————————————————————————— ■

The problem in our families, in our government, and in many businesses is that we have become so "sophisticated" in our thinking that we have lost sight of the basic elements. We behave as if these two basics were no longer relevant or necessary in our daily lives. Credit allows us to live in the short term, as if there were no bottom to the cookie jar and, therefore, no limit to our spending.

Deficit funding, at every level, has made the plan almost irrelevant because financing is always available to go beyond what was planned. The problem surfaces only when all sources of credit have dried up, and a life-style has been established far beyond the ability to repay. At this point, the options are so devastating that many couples end up in severe conflict which results in divorce or personal bankruptcy.

I have counseled many godly families in very desperate financial conditions because they had no plan for spending. And the opportunity to fund needs and greeds by using credit cards enabled them to overspend year after year when they ran out of credit, they had to make some tough decisions. Houses and cars had to be sold; children had to be taken out of private schools; clothing budgets had to be readjusted; and the total life-style had to undergo a dramatic reduction in order for them to survive, unless they wanted to declare bankruptcy. Declaring bankruptcy was not a real option, however, because they believe (as I do) that it is unbiblical.

Had they followed the basics of the cookie jar process or the envelope system, they never would have gotten into poor financial shape. Did these people *plan to fail?* No, they merely *failed to plan* and failed to choose to live within a plan. Debt is no man's friend; it will always make you a slave.

THE MECHANICS OF OUR SYSTEM

The system that we use with our children is very simple. Each child, beginning at about age eight, has been given a recipe file box containing five letter-sized envelopes: a "tithe" envelope, a "save" envelope, a "spend" envelope, a "gifts" envelope, and a "clothes" envelope.

The "spend" envelope contains money that can be used in any way they choose. The "gift" envelope is the amount allocated for buying gifts at Christmas, birthdays, and other special occasions for friends and relatives. The "clothes" amount is used to purchase *all* their clothes.

They are given a monthly allowance, in cash, to place in each of the envelopes according to a preset plan. The amount set for each envelope comes from an annual planning session that Judy and I have. We discuss the allowance amounts for each of the five categories, based on what they are required to pay for; then we give them one-twelfth of that amount each month in a lump sum.

Debt is no man's friend; it will always make you a slave.

As they earn money or as they receive gift money during the year, they deposit it into at least three envelopes, and perhaps all five envelopes. When they are beginning to learn about the system, they are required to put 10 percent into the "tithe" envelope and 10 percent into the "save" envelope; the balance can go into the "spend," "gift," and "clothes" envelopes. As they get older and understand the purpose of the system, they are given the freedom to divide the money as they see fit. We try to help them see the value and benefit of giving and saving. That way when they choose for themselves, they enjoy the experience of decision making.

The most important thing is not what children are responsible for buying, but how they handle the responsibility of managing the money.

Each family has to decide what children are responsible for in the various categories. The most important thing is not *what* children are responsible for buying, but how they handle the responsibility of managing the money. They need to know what they are responsible to buy, and that when the money is gone, there is no more. They must learn to live within the designated amount. If you want them to buy their own sports equipment, that's great. Allocate enough money to the "clothes" envelope so that they can cover those expenses, then require them to make the purchase.

If children habitually make the mistake of poor allocation—such as spending all of their money in October for fall clothes and, consequently, having no money left to buy the winter coat that is desperately needed—there are several ways to deal with this problem. First, you may decide to *not* make them responsible for what *you* consider to be the "necessities"—such as winter coats, snow boots, Sunday shoes, haircuts, school lunches, and so forth. *You* provide the money for those things. Second, you can let them do without. Third, they can live with the consequences of wearing last year's coat, shoes, or whatever. Fourth, you can make them earn the extra money needed for the purchase.

You come up with other creative alternatives, but the point is that children should have responsibility for certain budget items, and they must learn to allocate properly within those budget categories.

For a larger purchase, such as a bicycle, a tennis racquet, or a seasonal wardrobe, children may need several weeks or months before they accumulate enough to make the purchase. But when they have saved enough money and are ready to make the purchase, they can take the envelope with them and pay for the item with cash.

We allow them to borrow from envelope to envelope, except for the "tithe" and the "save" envelopes. They need to feel the responsibility for the management of the money, and therefore, we allow them a tremendous amount of flexibility in how they spend their money.

Their "save" envelope accumulates moneys that

they deposit periodically in a savings account in their name. As I mentioned earlier, at least once a year I will share with them how much money is in the savings account and show them how the interest causes that account to "grow" without their having to expend any physical or mental energy.

PRINCIPLES AND PRACTICES

Children can begin to manage money at a very early age. We believe that they can be given money to make decisions with, on their own, at age four or five. Perhaps they could have two or three envelopes—a "tithe" envelope, a "save" envelope, and a "spend" envelope.

By the time they have reached age eight or nine, we believe they can have all five envelopes and become responsible for planning and buying all their clothes and all the gifts they need to buy. The significant purchases—clothes and gifts—will require the greatest amount of discretion and thus provide the greatest value in training, right on through their college years. To say whether children can, or should, spend one hundred dollars per year or one thousand dollars per year on clothes is really a matter of the family and individual priorities and objectives.

When the children reach the teen years, they may choose to have more envelopes, and that is okay. However, we do not encourage our children to have more than six or seven envelopes until they reach college age. The system needs to be simple to work most efficiently.

We have included some completed sample budgets for a thirteen-year-old boy (Charts 5.1, 5.2, 5.3, 5.4) to help you determine how much allowance per budget category there will be. The amount per category will vary, first, by age, and second, by activities. We have found that even our children of the same sex have different financial requirements. Some children will spend more time participating in sports or taking music lessons than others; therefore, the budget amount should vary to recognize that. As children reach the teen years, they may have earnings they can use to meet some of the budget categories.

CHART 5.1
BUDGET WORKSHEET—CLOTHES
(Sample for 13-year-old boy)

	ESTIMATED ANNUAL AMOUNT (1)
I. CLOTHES	
A. Seasonal wardrobe	
1. Fall	$ 100
2. Winter	$ 150
3. Spring	$ 100
4. Summer	$ 75
B. Underwear and socks	$ 30
C. Shoes	
1. Dress	$ 100
2. Everyday	$ 135
3. Sports	$ 75
D. Coats	
1. Winter	$ 120
2. Spring	$ 75
E. Athletic clothes and equipment	$ 200
F. Accessories (ties, belts, jewelry)	$ 40
G. Other (band uniforms, stage costumes, etc.)	$ 0
	$ 0
	$ 0
	$ 0
	$ 0
Annual total	$ 1200 (2)
Monthly amount needed (annual total divided by 12)	$ 100 (3)
Subtract amount provided by allowance	(80) (4)
Amount to come from earnings and other sources	$ 20 (5)

1. *Estimate* annual amount for each category.
2. Add the amounts in all categories to get an annual total.
3. Divide the annual total (2) by 12 to get monthly amount.
4. Subtract the amount the parents will provide as a monthly allowance.
5. The monthly amount (3) less the allowance amount (4) results in the amount that must be provided from earnings, gifts, and other sources.

Parents need to make their decision whether a child should work while still in high school, based on their own unique circumstances and desires. Whatever the decision, it will impact the amount of the allowance. We did not require our two oldest daughters to work while they were participating in athletics or in cheerleading, but once the season was over we strongly encouraged them to get a job.

Each budget category needs to be reviewed for each child on a regular basis because circumstances and

CHART 5.2
BUDGET WORKSHEET—SPEND
(Sample for 13-year-old boy)

	ESTIMATED ANNUAL AMOUNT (1)	
II. SPEND		
A. Food and snacks (school lunches, other)	$ 480	
B. Entertainment (movies, sports, etc.)	$ 240	
C. Hobbies	$ 84	
D. Records/tapes	$ 60	
E. Jewelry	$ 0	
F. Personal grooming (haircuts, perms, supplies)	$ 48	
G. Reading material (books, magazine subscriptions)	$ 84	
H. School supplies	$ 24	
I. Auto		
1. Insurance	$ 0	
2. Gas, oil, maintenance	$ 0	
3. Repairs	$ 0	
4. Tires	$ 0	
Annual total	$ 1020	(2)
Monthly amount needed (annual total divided by 12)	$ 85	(3)
Subtract amount provided by allowance	(65)	(4)
Amount to come from earnings and other sources	$ 20	(5)

1. *Estimate* annual amount for each category.
2. Add the amounts in all categories to get an annual total.
3. Divide the annual total (2) by 12 to get monthly amount.
4. Subtract the amount the parents will provide as a monthly allowance.
5. The monthly amount (3) less the allowance amount (4) results in the amount that must be provided from earnings, gifts, and other sources.

needs will change. The budget categories we have presented are not the law. Give yourself time to determine the amounts needed. Be willing to make mistakes.

If this is the first time you have used this type of system, it may take a couple of years before you are comfortable with determining the amounts per category and even with the number of categories. At the end of this chapter are average amounts received and spent for all teens in 1990 according to the Nationwide Survey conducted by the Rand Youth Poll (Chart 5.5), which may be helpful to you in setting the amounts for your children.

CHART 5.3

BUDGET WORKSHEET—GIFTS
(Sample for 13-year-old boy)

III. GIFTS	ESTIMATED ANNUAL AMOUNT (1)		TOTAL (2)
	Family	Friends	
A. Christmas	$ 100	$ 20	$ 120
B. Birthdays	$ 100	$ 20	$ 120
C. Anniversaries	$ 10	$ 0	$ 10
D. Mother's/Father's Day	$ 20	$ 0	$ 20
E. Special Occasions			
1. Graduations	$ 10	$ 0	$ 10
2. Weddings	$ 0	$ 0	$ 0
3. Valentine's Day	$ 10	$ 10	$ 20
4. Easter	$ 0	$ 0	$ 0
5. Other	$ 0	$ 0	$ 0
F. Other	$ 0	$ 0	$ 0
Annual total	$ 250	$ 50	$ 300

Monthly amount needed (annual total divided by 12)	$ 25	(3)
Subtract amount provided by allowance	(15)	(4)
Amount to come from earnings and other sources	$ 10	(5)

1. *Estimate* annual amount for each category.
2. Add the amounts in all categories to get an annual total.
3. Divide the annual total (2) by 12 to get monthly amount.
4. Subtract the amount the parents will provide as a monthly allowance.
5. The monthly amount (3) less the allowance amount (4) results in the amount that must be provided from earnings, gifts, and other sources.

Those averages, however, do not include the total clothes budget for a child or any amount for a tithe. Therefore, your numbers will no doubt be higher in total than those averages. There are also two sets of blank forms you can use to begin the system. Remember, the *purpose* of the envelope system is not to have the system down pat, but to teach your children the basic tools of money management.

How frequently the allowance should be given will depend upon the ages of the children. If you begin the system with very young children, it probably should be given weekly because they cannot fully comprehend how much time is in a month or a year. When children reach age eight or nine, we believe that they should be given the money on a monthly basis. For example, their clothes money for the year is divided by twelve, and given to them monthly. They then have the responsibility for the money in the envelopes, the freedom of decision making, and the freedom to fail. Sometimes for clothes for our teenagers, we have given amounts on a semiannual or even annual basis in a lump sum, so that they can plan for and buy a wardrobe for a season.

The purpose of the envelope system is not to have the system down pat, but to teach your children the basic tools of money management.

Many parents are concerned that children will spend unwisely if they receive a large amount on a monthly basis. They may in the beginning, but that is how they are going to learn. After a series of mistakes, they will plan much more wisely. They must have the freedom to make their own decisions and the freedom to fail.

CHART 5.4

MONTHLY PLAN

(Sample for 13-year-old boy)

		MONTHLY AMOUNT NEEDED	ALLOWANCE	EARNINGS ETC.
Clothes	(1)	$ 100	$ 80	$ 20
Spend	l	$ 85	$ 65	$ 20
Gifts		$ 25	$ 15	$ 10
Total	(2)	$ 210	$ 160	$ 50
Save (10% of total)	(3)	$ 21	$ 16	$ 5
Tithe (10% of total)	(4)	$ 21	$ 16	$ 5
Total monthly plan	(5)	$ 252	$ 192	$ 60

1. Copy totals from appropriate Budget Worksheets for "monthly amount needed" [*worksheet line (3)*], "allowance" [*worksheet line (4)*], and "earnings, etc." [*worksheet line (5)*].
2. Add to get total for each category.
3. Multiply (2) by 10 percent (or another desired percentage).
4. Multiply (2) by 10 percent (or another desired percentage).
5. Add the total (2), the save (3), and the tithe (4) amounts to determine the total monthly plan.

Once the amount for each category has been determined and you are comfortable that it is a fair amount, you should not change it without a serious discussion. Our caution is to be wary of being manipulated by your children. If they learn that they can constantly change the amount by arguing, pouting, scheming, or just asking, the whole system of spending *limited* resources has been destroyed. In fact, there are no limits on the resources when you vary them according to the children's protests or desires.

The world is bent on teaching you and your children to get all you can *now*—no matter what the cost will be in the future. Both credit card companies and advertising firms have this motivation. You have an awesome job to try to teach your children delayed gratification through good money management and long-range planning. Don't

CHART 5.5
INCOME AND SPENDING

Boys Aged 13 Through 15

Income
Allowance	$15.25
Earnings	17.10
TOTAL	$32.35

Expenditures
Food and Snacks	$11.05
Clothing	6.05
Movies and Entertainment	4.80
Records	1.65
Personal Grooming	1.00
Hobbies	.85
Books, Paperbacks	.45
Magazines	.40
School Supplies	.35
Coin-operated Video Games	.20
Greeting Cards	.10
TOTAL	$26.90

Savings:
$5.45 a week towards athletic equipment, cameras, video games, radios, watches, computers, hand calculators, bicycles, and so on.

Note: The above and following figures on teen-age spending are based on weekly averages.

■ ────────────────────────── ■

The world is bent on teaching you and your children to get all you can now—no matter what the cost will be in the future.

■ ────────────────────────── ■

add to the problems they already face each day by allowing them to have unlimited resources to meet their wants and desires. Help them learn to be responsible, mature individuals by being able to put off today's desires for future benefits. On the other hand, remember to be flexible. There must be a proper balance.

Girls Aged 13 Through 15

Income

Allowance	$16.90
Earnings	18.80
TOTAL	$35.70

Expenditures

Clothing	$11.50
Food and Snacks	7.05
Movies and Entertainment	3.80
Cosmetics	3.60
Records	2.00
Jewelry	1.60
Fragrances	.55
Hair Products	.45
Beauty Parlor	.40
School Supplies	.40
Magazines	.35
Hobbies	.30
Books, Paperbacks	.25
Greeting Cards	.25
Coin-operated Video Games	.05
TOTAL	$32.55

Savings:

$3.15 a week towards radios, accessories, athletic equipment, bicycles, hand calculators, cameras, and so on.

A woman once explained the money management system she had her children using. I couldn't believe it—they were required to keep track of *every* penny they spent on a daily basis. That kind of record-keeping system would be appropriate for a CPA, but not for children. Her children rebelled against the rigidity of the system, which is not surprising.

Children should not be required to keep track of

Boys Aged 16 Through 19

Income

Allowance	$27.20
Earnings	47.05
TOTAL	$74.25

Expenditures

Clothing	$12.10
Movies, dating, entertainment	11.95
Food and Snacks	11.80
Gasoline and Auto	10.05
Personal Grooming	6.00
Records	1.60
Hobbies	1.15
Books, Paperbacks	.65
Magazines	.60
Coin-operated Video Games	.60
School Supplies	.45
Greeting Cards	.25
Cigarettes	.15
TOTAL	**$57.35**

Savings:

$16.90 a week towards education, motor vehicles, TV sets, computers, radios, hand calculators, video games, stereos, cameras, typewriters, sporting equipment, stocks, and so on.

where they spend the money within each envelope. The envelope is the record of how much they spent and how much is left. If children want to know why they are running out of money each month in a particular envelope and want to keep track of how they are spending it, that's fine; but they should not be required to keep track of every penny spent on a regular basis.

The amount given to children as an allowance should *definitely not* (1) *be withheld as a discipline* or *to influence behavior,* (2) *be based on performance of chores,* or (3) *vary once the agreed-upon amount has been determined to be fair and reasonable.*

This system is to teach children money management; it is not to be used, at the same time, as a discipli-

Girls Aged 16 Through 19

Income

Allowance	$28.80
Earnings	48.60
TOTAL	$77.40

Expenditures

Clothing	$25.90
Cosmetics	9.05
Food and Snacks	8.00
Movies and Entertainment	5.50
Gasoline and Auto	5.40
Jewelry	3.10
Records	2.30
Fragrances	2.00
Beauty Parlor	1.25
Hair Products	1.25
Books, Paperbacks	.85
Hobbies	.70
Magazines	.60
School Supplies	.50
Greeting Cards	.50
Cigarettes	.45
Coin-operated Video Games	.05
TOTAL	$67.40

Savings:

$10.00 a week towards education, marriage, vacations, travel, typewriters, hand calculators, cameras, radios, telephones, TV sets, and so on.

SOURCE: Nationwide Survey, Rand Youth Poll, 1990.

nary tool. For example, what happens if their grades go down? Do you take away their allowance? The answer is no. You are not using the system to motivate them to get good grades; there are other ways to accomplish those results.

CHART 5.6
BUDGET WORKSHEET—CLOTHES

I. CLOTHES	ESTIMATED ANNUAL AMOUNT (1)
A. Seasonal wardrobe	
1. Fall	$_____
2. Winter	$_____
3. Spring	$_____
4. Summer	$_____
B. Underwear and socks	$_____
C. Shoes	
1. Dress	$_____
2. Everyday	$_____
3. Sports	$_____
D. Coats	
1. Winter	$_____
2. Spring	$_____
E. Athletic clothes and equipment	$_____
F. Accessories (ties, belts, jewelry)	$_____
G. Other (band uniforms, stage costumes, etc.)	$_____
	$_____
	$_____
	$_____
	$_____
Annual total	$_____ (2)

Monthly amount needed (annual total divided by 12)	$_____ (3)
Subtract amount provided by allowance	(_____) (4)
Amount to come from earnings and other sources	$_____ (5)

1. *Estimate* annual amount for each category.
2. Add the amounts in all categories to get an annual total.
3. Divide the annual total (2) by 12 to get monthly amount.
4. Subtract the amount the parents will provide as a monthly allowance.
5. The monthly amount (3) less the allowance amount (4) results in the amount that must be provided from earnings, gifts, and other sources.

Also, the allowance is not a payment for chores. As we previously said, we believe that chores are of two types and are to be handled separately from teaching money management. Some chores are *expected;* as members of

CHART 5.7
BUDGET WORKSHEET—SPEND

	ESTIMATED ANNUAL AMOUNT (1)
II. SPEND	
A. Food and snacks (school lunches, other)	$_____
B. Entertainment (movies, sports, etc.)	$_____
C. Hobbies	$_____
D. Records/tapes	$_____
E. Jewelry	$_____
F. Personal grooming (haircuts, perms, supplies)	$_____
G. Reading material (books, magazine subscriptions)	$_____
H. School supplies	$_____
I. Autos	
1. Insurance	$_____
2. Gas, oil, maintenance	$_____
3. Repairs	$_____
4. Tires	$_____
Annual total	$_____ (2)
Monthly amount needed (annual total divided by 12)	$_____ (3)
Subtract amount provided by allowance	(_____) (4)
Amount to come from earnings and other sources	$_____ (5)

1. *Estimate* annual amount for each category.
2. Add the amounts in all categories to get an annual total.
3. Divide the annual total (2) by 12 to get monthly amount.
4. Subtract the amount the parents will provide as a monthly allowance.
5. The monthly amount (3) less the allowance amount (4) results in the amount that must be provided from earnings, gifts, and other sources.

the family, children should perform certain chores, such as doing the dishes, cleaning their room, making the bed, or carrying out the trash. Our children have to meet their responsibilities as members of the family, and one of those responsibilities is helping with chores around the house. We are a "team," and all members of the team must do their part. Others are *optional;* these chores are not expected of them, such as mowing the lawn, helping with the ironing, baby-sitting, or doing things above and beyond the normal expectations of the household.

As discussed earlier, it will take some time to come to a decision as to a fair and reasonable amount for the allowance. This may be as little as six months or as much as two years before you are sure of the amounts. Once the amount has been determined, however, you must not vary it, or you will teach children that there are, in reality, no boundaries. For that reason, we feel strongly that the amount should not be adjusted unless circumstances convince you that the amount is incorrect.

CHART 5.8
BUDGET WORKSHEET—GIFTS

III. GIFTS	ESTIMATED ANNUAL AMOUNT (1)		TOTAL (2)
	Family	Friends	
A. Christmas	$_____	$_____	$_____
B. Birthdays	$_____	$_____	$_____
C. Anniversaries	$_____	$_____	$_____
D. Mother's/Father's Day	$_____	$_____	$_____
E. Special Occasions			
1. Graduations	$_____	$_____	$_____
2. Weddings	$_____	$_____	$_____
3. Valentine's Day	$_____	$_____	$_____
4. Easter	$_____	$_____	$_____
5. Other	$_____	$_____	$_____
F. Other	$_____	$_____	$_____
Annual total	$_____	$_____	$_____

Monthly amount needed (annual total divided by 12)	$_____	(3)
Subtract amount provided by allowance	(_____)	(4)
Amount to come from earnings and other sources	$_____	(5)

1. *Estimate* annual amount for each category.
2. Add the amounts in all categories to get an annual total.
3. Divide the annual total (2) by 12 to get monthly amount.
4. Subtract the amount the parents will provide as a monthly allowance.
5. The monthly amount (3) less the allowance amount (4) results in the amount that must be provided from earnings, gifts, and other sources.

Once a year Judy and I take each child out to dinner as a birthday treat. During that dinner we discuss the child's goals for the next year as well as the goal accomplishments over the past year. To facilitate that conversation we keep a journal containing the goals. Those goals might be making a new friend, buying something of "significance," making certain grades in school, achieving something specific in a sport, or spending time daily reading God's Word.

CHART 5.9
MONTHLY PLAN

		MONTHLY AMOUNT NEEDED	ALLOWANCE	EARNINGS ETC.
Clothes	(1)	$____	$____	$____
Spend		$____	$____	$____
Gifts		$____	$____	$____
Total	(2)	$____	$____	$____
Save (10% of total)	(3)	$____	$____	$____
Tithe (10% of total)	(4)	$____	$____	$____
Total monthly plan	(5)	$____	$____	$____

1. Copy totals from appropriate Budget Worksheets for "monthly amount needed" [*worksheet line (3)*], "allowance" [*worksheet line (4)*], and "earnings, etc." [*worksheet line (5)*].
2. Add to get total for each category.
3. Multiply (2) by 10 percent (or another desired percentage).
4. Multiply (2) by 10 percent (or another desired percentage).
5. Add the total (2), the save (3), and the tithe (4) amounts to determine the total monthly plan.

We also review what the allowance will be for the next year for each of the five categories. We review the chores the child will be responsible for, both those that are *expected* and those that are *optional* for which they can earn compensation. If we did not set aside this predetermined time, which is extremely valuable but never urgent, we probably would not go through this process with each child.

CHART 5.10

BUDGET WORKSHEET—CLOTHES

	ESTIMATED ANNUAL AMOUNT (1)
I. CLOTHES	
A. Seasonal wardrobe	
1. Fall	$_____
2. Winter	$_____
3. Spring	$_____
4. Summer	$_____
B. Underwear and socks	$_____
C. Shoes	
1. Dress	$_____
2. Everyday	$_____
3. Sports	$_____
D. Coats	
1. Winter	$_____
2. Spring	$_____
E. Athletic clothes and equipment	$_____
F. Accessories (ties, belts, jewelry)	$_____
G. Other (band uniforms, stage costumes, etc.)	$_____
	$_____
	$_____
	$_____
	$_____
Annual total	$_____ (2)
Monthly amount needed (annual total divided by 12)	$_____ (3)
Subtract amount provided by allowance	(_____) (4)
Amount to come from earnings and other sources	$_____ (5)

1. *Estimate* annual amount for each category.
2. Add the amounts in all categories to get an annual total.
3. Divide the annual total (2) by 12 to get monthly amount.
4. Subtract the amount the parents will provide as a monthly allowance.
5. The monthly amount (3) less the allowance amount (4) results in the amount that must be provided from earnings, gifts, and other sources.

Of course, there is nothing biblical or magical about the birthday date, but it is a time that is special for each child. It is an occasion that few parents and virtually no children ever forget. With a large family it is easy to treat children as a group rather than as individuals. This technique allows us to deal with them individually in terms of their allowance, chores, and goals; it is very important to us that we treat each child as an individual.

WHAT THE SYSTEM TEACHES

The system we use is not the only system available. Feel free to take what we have shared and adapt it to your unique situation. We have found that the envelope system is a tool for teaching our children many things, and we have reviewed them here for you.

Tithing

In 1 Corinthians 16:2 we find the principles of giving, which are applicable for the New Testament church: "On the first day of the week let each one of you lay something aside, storing up as he may prosper, that there be no collections when I come."

The book of Proverbs says, "Honor the LORD with your possessions, / And with the firstfruits of all your increase; / So your barns will be filled with plenty, / And your vats will overflow with new wine" (3:9–10).

The tithe is the recognition that God owns it all. If your children put money into a "tithe" envelope on a regular basis and then give it, they are learning the habit of tithing. This will become ingrained in their minds as recognition that God owns it all.

Rewards for Work

By having a limited supply of money, children must earn additional money for the discretionary items they want. Then when they make a purchase, they are learning a significant reward for work.

Savings

Saving teaches the principle of delayed gratification. Putting money into a "save" envelope on a regular basis is an important discipline to ensure financial success. Allowing some of the savings amount to be spent periodically for significant items will begin to teach delayed gratification. Remember the definition of financial maturity—"giving up today's desires for future benefits."

Opportunity Cost of Consumption

When the money is gone, you cannot buy anything else. There is no more dramatic way to teach the opportunity cost of consumption. The cost is not dollar-for-dollar, but multiple dollars taken out of the future that could have been available had the money not been spent. The system makes that principle a reality.

> *God is the only One who never has, and never will, exhaust His resources.*

Limited Supply of Money

The whole system is built around the principle that there is a limited supply of money. When the cookie jar or the envelope is empty, the only way to get funds is to work. Contrary to the world's philosophy, there is an end to what can be spent. God is the only One who never has, and never will, exhaust His resources.

Decision Making

Dealing with a limited number of resources and an unlimited number of choices on which to spend those resources requires that decisions be made.

Budgeting

Budgeting is a one-year financial plan, and the whole system is built as a one-year financial plan.

Wise Buying

Children do not have to be wise buyers for the system to work, but they will quickly learn that by buying wisely they will have more money available to do other things.

CHART 5.11
BUDGET WORKSHEET—SPEND

II. SPEND	ESTIMATED ANNUAL AMOUNT (1)	
A. Food and snacks (school lunches, other)	$_____	
B. Entertainment (movies, sports, etc.)	$_____	
C. Hobbies	$_____	
D. Records/tapes	$_____	
E. Jewelry	$_____	
F. Personal grooming (haircuts, perms, supplies)	$_____	
G. Reading material (books, magazine subscriptions)	$_____	
H. School supplies	$_____	
I. Autos		
1. Insurance	$_____	
2. Gas, oil, maintenance	$_____	
3. Repairs	$_____	
4. Tires	$_____	
Annual total	$_____	(2)
Monthly amount needed (annual total divided by 12)	$_____	(3)
Subtract amount provided by allowance	(_____)	(4)
Amount to come from earnings and other sources	$_____	(5)

1. *Estimate* annual amount for each category.
2. Add the amounts in all categories to get an annual total.
3. Divide the annual total (2) by 12 to get monthly amount.
4. Subtract the amount the parents will provide as a monthly allowance.
5. The monthly amount (3) less the allowance amount (4) results in the amount that must be provided from earnings, gifts, and other sources.

Goal Setting

Our boys began realizing at ages 9 and 11 that if they do not spend the money they earn during the summers they will have saved enough money to buy a car when they are age sixteen. The system teaches the wisdom and value of setting long-term as well as short-term goals.

CHART 5.12
BUDGET WORKSHEET—GIFTS

III. GIFTS	ESTIMATED ANNUAL AMOUNT (1)		TOTAL (2)
	Family	Friends	
A. Christmas	$_____	$_____	$_____
B. Birthdays	$_____	$_____	$_____
C. Anniversaries	$_____	$_____	$_____
D. Mother's/Father's Day	$_____	$_____	$_____
E. Special Occasions			
1. Graduations	$_____	$_____	$_____
2. Weddings	$_____	$_____	$_____
3. Valentine's Day	$_____	$_____	$_____
4. Easter	$_____	$_____	$_____
5. Other	$_____	$_____	$_____
F. Other	$_____	$_____	$_____
Annual total	$_____	$_____	$_____

Monthly amount needed (annual total divided by 12)	$_____	(3)
Subtract amount provided by allowance	(_____)	(4)
Amount to come from earnings and other sources	$_____	(5)

1. *Estimate* annual amount for each category.
2. Add the amounts in all categories to get an annual total.
3. Divide the annual total (2) by 12 to get monthly amount.
4. Subtract the amount the parents will provide as a monthly allowance.
5. The monthly amount (3) less the allowance amount (4) results in the amount that must be provided from earnings, gifts, and other sources.

CONCLUSION

The most critical issue regarding the envelope system is that children must have *goal ownership*. In other words, it must be *their* system rather than your system imposed upon them. Help them set up the system and understand what they can learn it. Then allow them to have control of the money and freedom to work within the system.

Children may change the system to fit their needs. Karen was having trouble with the system when she was ten or eleven years old because she prefers to live spontaneously, and our system made her feel too confined. She told Judy that she was fed up with the envelope system. As Judy talked with her, she discovered that Karen did not "feel" free to spend. She was trying to live, if you will, under the law. What she really wanted was to have some money to "flit" away if she chose to do so.

Judy, with great wisdom, suggested to her that she add a sixth envelope and call it her "flit" envelope. Money in the flit envelope could be used any way that she chose. In reality, she had that freedom with her "spend" envelope, but she didn't feel the freedom. Merely by setting up another envelope and labeling it the way she wanted, she experienced tremendous freedom to operate within the system.

Money is nothing more than a resource, and money management is nothing more than a tool to use that resource.

Although she does not enjoy discipline as a way of life, Karen has become a very disciplined young lady in certain necessary areas of her life—her school work and her money management. She does an excellent job of managing her money, and I believe that is because she had the freedom to learn when she was allowed to design the system. The "flit" envelope taught me something I needed to remember: Money is nothing more than a resource, and money management is nothing more than a tool to use that resource. Neither is an end in itself!

Our challenge to you is as follows:

1. Discuss the system with your children and make sure they understand the extent of their responsibility.

2. Review the Budget Worksheets and set the allowance amounts for each of your children.

3. Give your children the file box with the money already inserted in the envelopes for the first month.

4. Be flexible!

5. Watch your children take responsibility for this very important area of their lives.

CHART 5.13
MONTHLY PLAN

		MONTHLY AMOUNT NEEDED	ALLOWANCE	EARNINGS ETC.
Clothes (1)		$____	$____	$____
Spend ǀ		$____	$____	$____
Gifts		$____	$____	$____
Total	(2)	$____	$____	$____
Save (10% of total)	(3)	$____	$____	$____
Tithe (10% of total)	(4)	$____	$____	$____
Total monthly plan	(5)	$____	$____	$____

1. Copy totals from appropriate Budget Worksheets for "monthly amount needed" [*worksheet line (3)*], "allowance" [*worksheet line (4)*], and "earnings, etc." [*worksheet line (5)*].
2. Add to get total for each category.
3. Multiply (2) by 10 percent (or another desired percentage).
4. Multiply (2) by 10 percent (or another desired percentage).
5. Add the total (2), the save (3), and the tithe (4) amounts to determine the total monthly plan.

The System Continued

O ur fourth child and oldest boy, Tim has been on the envelope system for several years now. One summer many years ago, Judy mentioned that Tim needed a new pair of trousers for our vacation. His response was simply, "I don't have any more money left in my clothes envelope." He wasn't disappointed or angry that he had no more money; it was just a fact. He didn't even try to convince her to buy the trousers. It was his responsibility, and he would take care of it when he had the money. His timing was not necessarily our timing, but that is a part of what it means to live in a family.

In addition to the envelope system, there are other effective and necessary how-to's. We have learned many of these how-to's from others, and we hope that you, too, can find something useful here.

OTHER HOW-TO'S

1. Family Conferences

One of the most important how-to's is the family conference. Family conferences can be both planned and unplanned, but probably the best teaching time is the unplanned conference. Most of the time these occur around the dinner table, but on some occasions we call a special family conference.

For example, we have had several conferences to discuss the financial requests we get from charitable organizations and from individuals. Our family has often had the opportunity to meet the financial needs of a specific family or friend that our children have brought to our attention. In some cases we have helped one child's classmates on a summer mission trip; in other instances we have assisted a family in need.

I remember on one occasion we discussed a young boy who had come to school without any winter clothes because his family could not afford them. This conference took place during the winter, and the need was immediate. I had a new nylon ski jacket, which I really enjoyed because it was the first jacket that really kept me warm on cold wintry days. I felt a sense of conviction during our conference to give that jacket to the boy, but not until there was a substantial tug between what I really wanted to do and what I felt I needed to do. I gave that jacket because I felt God would have me to do that. I did not do it to make a teaching point, but it did, without question, have an effect on our children.

Many times at our family conferences we will discuss family activities and their cost. For some time we have been discussing the vacations we would like to take. As a matter of fact, it has become a joke that at every family conference we must talk about the vacation.

We may talk about major decisions that are confronting members of the family or that involve the whole family. We enjoy thinking through major decisions together such as school changes, housing relocation, and career opportunities.

The family conference does several things. First, it teaches that family members have different priorities. Just because someone is a member of a family does not automatically give him the same set of priorities as the rest of the family. Second, it also teaches the decision making process that we will talk about in chapter 12. Many times during these discussions we will actually go through the formal decision-making process.

Third, children learn during these times that parents don't have all the answers, and they do make mistakes. To be willing to be taught by your children demonstrates to them an important principle of life, and that is the value of teachability. If children can leave home having seen teachability in their parents and having learned to be teachable themselves, they are set up for lives of success.

■ ──────────────────────────────── ■

To be willing to be taught by your children demonstrates to them an important principle of life, and that is the value of teachability.

■ ──────────────────────────────── ■

Judy and I have learned as much, I am sure, from our children as they have learned from us. We have found them to be very wise counselors. When we have a major decision to make, we frequently go to them, either in a family conference or individually, to get their advice and counsel. I even share business problems and decisions that need to be made on a regular basis, and especially when it comes to "people" problems, I have found the children to be wise counselors.

2. Releasing the Children

Another how-to involves a dinner on their eighteenth birthday. We do this to celebrate the birthday but, more importantly, to formalize a time of releasing them. We tell them that we have done the best job we could in teaching, counseling, and raising them. We explain that they are now at the age of personal accountability, and our role in their lives changes from that of rule maker to that of friend and counselor. We advise them that all decisions in life from that point are theirs. We will help them if they ask us, but we will not make their decisions for them.

If they continue to live with us, if only during the summers and vacation times, we ask them to abide by the rules of our household. These rules are very simple and basic, such as being at dinner on time, using the facilities in consideration of others, and maintaining their rooms in an orderly manner. When they come in, whom they date, and so on are their decisions.

Also, during that celebration dinner we preview how we will be of assistance to them financially. We tell them what expenses we will pay for regarding college; anything above and beyond that is their responsibility. We advise them how we will be responsible for expenses of graduate school if they desire to go on for an advanced degree. We tell them what assistance to expect regarding automobiles and marriage expenses. We also tell them what we will be available to do for them after marriage.

None of these decisions regarding financial assistance are unique to us. However, we have made these decisions, in advance. We hope we have effectively communicated them to the children so that they can accept the responsibility to plan and manage their lives in accordance with their goals, priorities, commitments, and objectives.

We remind them that we will always be available for assistance and counsel on both major and minor decisions. But we make it clear that we will not, to the best of our ability, interfere in their lives. Whom they marry, how they raise their children, where they live, and how they manage their money are their decisions.

The first response of our three daughters who have gone through this process has been one of fright to think of being personally accountable, but they have handled the responsibility extremely well. We feel that the formal release is very important for them to begin to feel the burden of responsibility to make their own decisions.

It is a strange phenomenon with teenagers. They desire freedom, but when they really get it, they tend to return to their roots because it is a fearful thing. They are not necessarily trying to gain freedom as much as looking to be treated as responsible human beings.

3. Denial of Wants and Desires

Above and beyond the basic needs of life, financially or in other areas, everyone has wants and desires. Children, it seems, have a bottomless pit of wants and desires. They want a candy bar every time they are in a store. They want to stop for an ice-cream cone every time they are out in the car. They want the newest dress, baseball glove, tennis racquet, pair of shoes, cars, and on and on. Where is the limit? The envelope system sets the limits for most of the financial needs of children. However, to be realistic, we must recognize their continuous demands for impulse purchases.

The real issue concerns boundaries of spending, not whether or not we can afford something. Many times we say no just to remind ourselves and our children that there is not a bottomless pit of money available to be spent. We must teach this fundamental principle to our children and live by it as parents.

However, we do not always deny them. We feel free to say yes at certain times if for no other reason than to teach flexibility instead of rigidity. First Timothy 6:17 says, "Command those who are rich in this present age not to be haughty, nor to trust in uncertain riches but in the living God, *who gives richly all things to enjoy*" (emphasis added). The Christian life is not meant to be a life of rigidity, and as parents, we need to model the freedom of being in Christ. But please do not interpret this to mean that we have liberty to do whatever we please. We are saying that in living the Christian life, spontaneity and freedom are not only allowed but also encouraged by our Lord.

■ ─────────────────────────────── ■

Children, it seems, have a bottomless pit of wants and desires.

■ ─────────────────────────────── ■

The denial of wants and desires teaches children many things, including the truth that there are boundaries in life, and all of us need those boundaries. As strange as it may seem, boundaries are freeing. When we know where the limits are, we can enjoy moving around within them. Let us explain this a bit further.

■ ─────────────────────────────── ■

As strange as it may seem, boundaries are freeing. When we know where the limits are, we can enjoy moving around within them.

■ ─────────────────────────────── ■

A study was done of preschoolers whose nursery school playground extended all the way to a very busy street. For the first two months of school there was no fence around it, and all the children stayed huddled near the school building because they were afraid of the traffic. However, after a fence was installed, the children played all the way out to the boundaries it provided. They were no longer afraid of the traffic, and they loved the freedom they had within the confines of the fence. As adults, we need boundaries in our lives just as surely as these children did and just as surely as our children do.

The denial of wants and desires also teaches accountability. We are accountable first to God and then to those with whom we live. The willingness to deny ourselves because God commands it, or because it is best for us and our family, helps us realize that we are accountable to someone else. R. C. Sproul has said, "If there is no accountability, then one's life is of no account."

4. Freedom to Fail

Again we want to remind you that children must have the freedom to fail. This is the most valuable way they can learn. Please do not deny them that freedom. Allow them to make decisions that you know to be wrong. Obviously, we are not talking about decisions that will be harmful to them. However, many decisions are wrong financially, but in the long run, they are inexpensive when it comes to the lessons learned. Some wrong financial decisions that are not too costly would be buying extremely faddish clothes, purchasing easily-broken toys, or spending money for food foolishly at shows and amusement parks at the cost of a better use of that money.

■ ─────────────────────────────────────── ■

How we handle failure is critical for developing the maturity to live well.

■ ─────────────────────────────────────── ■

5. Model Failure and Success

It is just as important to model failure for them as it is to model success. All of us have had failures in our lives. How we handle failure is critical for developing the maturity to live well.

Financial success, on the other hand, may be more difficult to handle than failure. For every person who can handle success, there are ten who can handle failure. When you have failed, you generally have no alternative but to pick up the pieces and go on.

When you are successful, the number of alternatives to make mistakes increases almost geometrically; therefore, success is more difficult to handle. Maintaining balance in your life when you are successful becomes increasingly difficult. For example, giving 20 percent of your income when you are in college may mean very little in terms of gross dollars, but giving 20 percent when your income reaches one hundred thousand dollars becomes very difficult because of the alternative uses of that larger amount of money.

Your failures to handle money wisely can be the mistake you have made with a limited amount of money or those you have made with surplus capital. The amount is less significant than your response to the failure. In either event it is important for your children to know how you handled the situation.

■ ────────────────────────────────────── ■

Failures should be treated as positive learning experiences.

■ ────────────────────────────────────── ■

I have made many really stupid financial decisions throughout my life. The most important thing in teaching your children about your failures is that failures should be treated as positive learning experiences. Don't become defensive about them. Admit the mistakes; tell what you learned from them and go on.

I remember all too well impulsively buying a used car to replace one of our other automobiles. I went against my experience, good judgment, and wife's advice to purchase this car, primarily because I wanted it. We still have that car, but it has been, it seems, a bottomless hole of repairs and maintenance. My children know how the mistake was made and why the mistake was made, and unfortunately they have a visual reminder every day that Dad makes some really stupid financial decisions every now and then.

We will all experience financial failures in one form or another. How we model that failure to our children is a valuable teaching lesson.

6. As You Go

Jesus continually taught His disciples as they went. It did not matter if they were in the middle of a field, in the temple, or at sea in a boat. He used ordinary happenings to teach them.

The best time for teaching to take place is when the pupils are willing to learn and can relate to what is being taught right then. This principle holds true when teaching children, also. Children should be taught as you go— as you go shopping, as you go on vacation, as you go to church, as you go wherever. Don't miss the opportunities to teach.

■ ─────────────────────────────── ■

Children should be taught as you go—as you go shopping, as you go on vacation, as you go to church, as you go wherever.

■ ─────────────────────────────── ■

To sit children down and say, "Now you are going to learn how to buy a shirt wisely," is not the most effective way to teach how to buy a shirt. The best way to teach that is to be with them when they are buying one. The best time to teach how to save money by doing repairs is when repairs have to be made; and they can learn from you and with you.

To be able to teach your children "as you go" requires that you listen to them. When I say "listen," I don't mean to listen to just their words. Listen to the meanings and feelings behind the words. What are they really saying? Why are they saying it? How can you best respond to them in words they can understand? This type of listening means you are tuned in to them rather than to what is going on at the office or what is on your calendar for tonight or tomorrow. It means being where they are mentally as well as physically.

By not listening to what is said, we can miss spontaneous teaching opportunity. In our home Judy does that much better than I am. It requires a constant choice on my part to listen to what they are really saying. I find that when I do, I am able to teach in the daily course of life. Very seldom in such instances have I set out to teach something on purpose.

Effective communication is both consistent and repetitive.

CONCLUSION

We learned long ago that effective communication is both consistent and repetitive. We trust that this book has been consistent throughout, and we are sure that you have found it to be repetitive in some cases. The reason for this is that our goal is to communicate to you the principles and practices necessary for you and for your children to be effective money managers.

The same two requirements are necessary in raising children and communicating to them what they need to know. You must be consistent in your communication, and without question, you must be repetitive. Will they learn overnight? Absolutely not! But do not give up. The rewards of having children effectively managing their money while they are in high school, before they leave home, is well worth the cost of being consistent and repetitive in your communication.

In Chapter 4 we stated our belief that child must learn four basic principles and four basic skills for successful money management. In that chapter we discussed the first principle, the fact that God owns it all. With that foundation, we are now ready to examine the other principles and skills which are part of your children's training process. Part 3 will show how understanding each of these will ultimately help your child achieve financial responsibility. Along the way, we will answer some of the specific questions you probably have about how the money management system works.

Remember again, principles are taught; skills must be taught.

Part 3

■————————————————————■

The Results

An Old-Time Value—Work

Imagine yourself for the moment as a child between the ages of two and ten. As you have wants, needs, and desires, you go to your parents with your requests. For example, you want a soft drink at a ball game or an amusement park, an irresistible stuffed animal, a yummy candy bar, a super-duper bicycle, whatever it is. At first you ask for it. If one parent ignores you or turns you down, you quickly learn that the other parent may be a source; or if you demand loudly enough, long enough, and in the right way, perhaps you will get what you want.

A child learns many things this way. He learns how to manipulate. Even more devastating than that, he learns there is no limit to the money supply. At least that is how it seems to the child, even though it is not true. Most parents have said (probably many times), "Don't you know that money doesn't grow on trees?" But why should a child believe there is a problem with the supply of money? There always seems to be more if the right "technique" is used to obtain it.

THE SOMETHING-FOR-NOTHING ILLUSION

Many adults have the same mistaken belief. Each of us grows up wanting something for nothing. Witness, if you will, the growth in the number of state lotteries. States have learned that, even against overwhelming odds, people will make a foolish financial decision by participating in a lottery with the hope of getting something for nothing. The reality is, however, that all financial resources cost somebody something. There is no such thing as "a free lunch." Yet we learn from an early age that perhaps there really is something for nothing, and many of us spend a lifetime pursuing that illusion.

Each of us grows up wanting something for nothing.

Even in the simplest economic system, one thing of value is traded for something else of equal value. Value is in the mind of the beholder, and the price merely reflects the value. For example, one person may trade a day's labor for one hundred dollars, and another person may trade a day's labor for something more or less. One person may trade many days of labor for an automobile, and others may trade those same days of labor for a vacation. The "value" of that trade-off is in the eye of the beholder.

THE COST/BENEFIT TRADE-OFF

The second basic principle that must be caught by children is that there is a trade-off between time-and-effort (cost), and money-and-rewards (benefit). In reality money does not grow on trees, and there is no free lunch. Every purchase costs either parents or children something in terms of labor.

In addition to provide economically for ourselves,

we must work for two other important reasons: (1) we are commanded to work, and (2) there is an intrinsic value in work. The Bible says, "Let him who stole steal no longer, but rather let him labor, working with his hands what is good, that he may have something to give him who has need" (Eph. 4:28). We are commanded to work so that we will have the ability to give to others.

Proverbs 14:23 states, "In all labor there is profit, / But idle chatter leads only to poverty." Working has intrinsic value; it brings monetary rewards as well as the satisfaction of knowing a job has been done well and completed. For that reason alone it is profitable to work. Having known many people who are financially independent, I have yet to see any who are happy unless they also have some meaningful work to accomplish. God has built into us the need to work.

Second Thessalonians records Paul's words: "Nor did we eat anyone's bread free of charge, but worked with labor and toil night and day, that we might not be a burden to any of you, not because we do not have authority, but to make ourselves an example of how you should follow us" (3:8–9). Even though he could have legitimately requested support from the church at Thessalonica, Paul wanted to be an example and show them the value of providing for oneself. Obviously, these verses convey how important it is for us and our children to learn the rewards of labor.

MOTIVATION

The really difficult problem for parents, however, is figuring out how to motivate children to work. I will never forget the thrill of learning our oldest daughter, Cynthia, had taken the initiative to find a summer job between her freshman and sophomore years in college. She and I had not even discussed looking for a job. But to know that she saw the necessity to work, then determined to find a job, was of tremendous satisfaction to me. I was even more impressed when I found out that she had contacted my own company as well as several others in Atlanta.

I don't claim to have all the answers as to how to motivate children to work, but I can offer some advice that seems to be effective. First, I believe children must experience the benefits of working early in life. In other words, when they are required to work, they experience the intrinsic value of working and feel good about a job well done. That self-satisfaction provides the motivation to work, and so it is a self-perpetuating process. Additionally, they must experience the satisfaction of obedience. They shouldn't be paid for every job they do around the house. Work has a benefit, in and of itself, that is above and beyond the economic benefit of working; and it is important, as a part of the training process, for them to experience this benefit. It can only happen if they are required to work, doing chores around the house, without receiving pay.

■ —————————————————————————————————— ■

Working has intrinsic value; it brings monetary rewards as well as the reward that comes from the satisfaction of knowing a job has been done well and completed.

■ —————————————————————————————————— ■

On the other hand, they should be paid for doing certain chores so that they can experience the economic benefit of working. This benefit comes from learning that money will provide something they really desire.

Second, in addition to experiencing early the benefits of working—its intrinsic value, the satisfaction of obedience, and the economic rewards—children can be motivated to work because they get some time with one parent or both parents.

We have a rule in our home that everyone helps to clear the table and do the dishes after meals. No one is permitted to leave the kitchen until it is clean. The boys typically grumble some—I think more out of a feeling that they *should* rather than out of any heartfelt feeling of mistreatment. The task passes quickly with the unified effort, made livelier with playful jesting and a little sibling competition. And working alongside Judy and me seems to provide encouragement and motivation for them to learn.

POSITIVE FEEDBACK

Third, children must receive positive feedback in the form of encouragement. As they are complimented for the work they do, they learn that there is a reward to work.

Telling children about the benefits of work, without giving them the opportunity to work, is of no value whatsoever.

When I train my children in some task, lawn work for example, I am tempted to be critical because the job is not done to my specifications. But I must put the initial poor performance into perspective. I am trying to teach them the rewards for work so that they will be motivated to work. Will my criticism of them while they are learning *how to work* keep them from *wanting to work?* So, I must encourage them based on where they are in the learning process.

Judy and I know some things won't work because we have experienced them. Telling children about the benefits of work, without giving them the opportunity to work, is of no value whatsoever. Trying to motivate them to work by making them feel guilty creates resistance and negative feelings. This approach has not been successful with our children. Bribing them to work by the promise of economic reward may get the job accomplished, but that method will never teach children the intrinsic value of work.

CHORES AND ALLOWANCES

What chores should you require your children to perform? At what age should they begin those chores? How should you use allowances in this whole process? These are some of the difficult questions you face. Judy and I think that a good place to start is to establish guidelines for chores, allowances, and work for compensation.

They have chores because they are members of the family, and they receive allowances because they are members of the family. The two are not dependent on each other.

Our children must perform certain chores just because they are members of our family. They must assume part of the responsibility for living in our household. These chores are keeping a clean room, helping with the dishes, helping with the cleaning, laundry, and so on. They receive no payment for doing these chores and these chores begin at a very early age. The chores increase in scope as the children get older.

By the same token, our children receive allowances strictly because they have needs and are members of the family. In other words, we do not tie together the payment of an allowance with the completion of chores. They have chores because they are members of the family, and they receive allowances because they are members of the family. The two are not dependent on each other.

In addition to required chores, certain jobs around the house are optional, and they receive compensation for these jobs. Perhaps it is helping with the ironing, washing a car, or baby-sitting, but the job is not a requirement. Therefore, they learn that they can earn extra money, but they must trade time for the money, which, in turn, will purchase something.

We find that for them to work strictly to earn money to save is not something that comes naturally. They almost always will work to earn money to buy something they need *now*. This motivation is okay, however, because we are attempting to teach them that there is a trade-off between time-and-effort and money-and-rewards by providing them with that opportunity. The long-term perspective will come later.

GIFTS

In addition to allowances and payment for jobs, we periodically feel the freedom to give our children money for no reason whatsoever. We do this because our heavenly Father gives us gifts we don't earn or deserve. This is called grace. All the economic resources that we ultimately end up with are gifts from God. As parents, we want our children to understand that God is a gracious God, and He may choose to give us gifts for no reason whatsoever.

Make no mistake about it. A gift is not the same thing as a handout. A handout comes because children beg for it or use another form of manipulation. A gift is unasked for, unearned and, often, undeserved.

Grandparents many times destroy what parents are attempting to teach children because they overuse handouts. They become a form of manipulation.

I have seen overindulgence many times among the wealthy. Oftentimes, a wealthy grandparent chooses to use good tax planning to set up trusts for grandchildren. In many cases, these trusts may be enough to make the child financially independent as early as age twenty-one. When a child knows for certain that at a young age, he or she will be financially independent, there is often little the parents can do to teach responsible money management. The child may adopt the prevailing attitude that work is unimportant and that the money will always be there. I know of one wealthy family whose grandparent set up trusts that won't expire until the year 2047. There was so much money in this family that the third, fourth and even fifth generation will be financially independent. That grandparent has made it extremely difficult for his children and grandchildren, to be able to teach their own children the value of work.

However, overindulgence can take place with those who have less than enough to make their grandchildren financially independent. It can be in the form of birthday gifts, Christmas gifts, entertainment or cars. A grandparent needs to be very careful not to thwart the efforts of their own children who are attempting to train *their* children.

Our challenge to grandparents and future grandparents is threefold. First, think of what you are teaching grandchildren by giving them handouts. Second, consider your real motive for giving the handout. Is it to gain favor with the children at the cost of teaching them absolutely the wrong thing regarding money? Third, remember that money will never replace your time with them.

Teaching children to work is part of looking out for their best interests, now in childhood and later in adulthood. It is the same thing as *teaching* a man to fish rather than *giving* him a fish. Once you have taught him to fish, you have given him the gift of feeding himself for the rest of his life. Giving him a fish when he is hungry lasts for just a few hours. Teaching children to work equips them for any economic situation and sets them up to lead lives of satisfaction. What a gift to give to your children!

You Can't Have Everything

Income has facetiously been defined as something you can't live without or within. Our daughter Karen's problem of how to spend her limited resources, mentioned in Chapter 1, is the same problem each of us faces every day.

Some solve the problems as she did. We started our shopping trip at a toy store where she found what she had planned to buy, a pair of skates. While standing in line to pay for them, suddenly she decided to do a little more shopping. As we walked through the shopping center, she went into a store that sold small gifts, candy, notions, and party favors. Within just a few minutes she had impulsively selected several items and spent most of her money, certainly not leaving enough to buy the skates. The next day what she had bought was broken, used up, or of no real value anymore.

Karen experienced the frustration of having to actually allocate her limited resources among unlimited alternatives. *Once the final decision is made, it is forever made.* As she has reminded me many times since then, the longer term the perspective, the better the financial decision made today.

Confronted with the dilemma of limited financial

resources to meet all our desires, needs, and wants, we buy on impulse or out of total frustration. We buy because we don't know how to allocate the money, or at the other extreme, we experience analysis paralysis. That means we spend so much time analyzing the decision that we never make the decision, or if we do make it, we are forever afterward concerned that we could have made a better decision.

It is no wonder many of us spend our lives feeling guilty because of the way we make financial decisions. Nor is it any wonder frustration results because we have so many choices available to us on a daily basis. This problem is not uniquely American, but it is certainly accentuated in America, as any citizen of a Third World country will tell you. Only in America are there forty-two kinds of cereal to choose from or fifty different types of toothpaste, packaged in five different ways.

Adults have basically five uses for money: tithing, paying taxes, repaying debt, spending for life-style, or saving for the future. Children, for the most part, have only three uses for money since they do not have to pay taxes and rarely do they have debt to repay.

■ ─────────────────────────────────── ■

All of us have goals. Whether or not we have recognized them as goals is another question.

■ ─────────────────────────────────── ■

The allocation among these spending alternatives is a function of three things: goals, commitments, and priorities. All of us have goals. Whether or not we have recognized them as goals is another question. A changed life-style can be a goal; to be debt-free can be a goal; to be financially independent can also be a goal. Commitments, of course, are just that; biblically we have no choice but to honor our commitments. Debt is probably the most significant commitment that we take on other than family commitments. As parents of five children, we obviously have certain life-style commitments, such as more food, a larger home, different transportation needs, and so on, than a family with only one child. Children have very few commitments, so how they allocate their money will largely be a matter of priorities and individual goals.

BIBLICAL PRIORITIES

The Bible speaks to the five uses of money. From what God's Word has to say, I believe that we can set our own spending priorities. Looking at each of the areas individually, but certainly not attempting to exhaust our study of Scripture, we can see the following priorities:

1. Giving

"On the first day of the week let each of you lay something aside, storing up as he may prosper, that there be no collections when I come" (1 Cor. 16:2). Paul's commandment is to regularly, on the first day of the week, give in the amount as God has prospered. How much that is depends, we believe, on what God would have you to do, but no less than a tithe amount.

■ ——————————————————————————— ■

For the Christian, nonpayment of debt is not an option.

■ ——————————————————————————— ■

2. Paying Taxes

Jesus said, "Render therefore to Caesar the things that are Caesar's, and to God the things that are God's"

(Luke 20:25). The payment of taxes is a biblical commandment; therefore, any cheating or falsification of tax information is an act of disobedience to God.

3. Repaying Debt

"The wicked borrows and does not repay, / But the f debt is not an option, for that individual is called wicked. Christian, nonpayment of debt is not an option, for that individual is called wicked.

Tithing, paying taxes, and repaying debt are biblical priorities *before any other spending of income.* In financial planning, there is a concept of *net spendable income,* which is the total (or gross) income less amounts for tithe, taxes, and debt repayment. The balance is left for the other two priorities—spending and saving. Too often spending becomes the first priority, and the biblical priorities are ignored.

If family members would consider that the only amount available to spend is the amount left after the tithe, taxes, and debt repayment, in many cases they would radically reduce their life-style. In the long term, they would also radically improve their total financial situation.

The only way to reduce life-style is to make conscious, item-by-item decisions to reduce or eliminate expenses, such as eating out less, using fewer prepared foods, taking children out of private schools, moving into a smaller home, keeping a car longer, doing repairs and maintenance yourself, taking less expensive vacations, or buying less expensive clothes. What you do or not do is always a matter of personal choice that will not come from your own priorities and desires, but the bottom line is that the only amount available to spend is the amount left after the tithe, taxes, and debt repayment.

This priority system will enhance the ability to provide for those productive, long-term uses. The dollars saved by reducing life-style flow directly to the bottom line of cash available for productive, long-term uses, such as college education, home purchase, debt retirement, or savings.

■ ──────────────────────────────── ■

The dollars saved by reducing life-style flow directly to the bottom line of cash available for productive, long-term uses.

■ ──────────────────────────────── ■

4. Spending

First Timothy states, "Command those who are rich in this present age not to be haughty, nor to trust in uncertain riches but in the living God, who gives us richly all things to enjoy. Let them do good, that they be rich in good works, ready to give, willing to share" (6:17–18). In other words, God wants us to enjoy what He has blessed us with, but those things are not to become our gods. We should hold with an open hand what He has entrusted to us, ready to share with those in need. If we spend everything on ourselves, we cannot be faithful to these verses.

5. Saving

Proverbs 13:11 reminds us: "He who gathers money little by little causes it to grow" (NIV). The key to financial success is to spend less than is earned and continue to do that for a lengthy period of time. That family, without question, will be financially secure in the long term. However, they must give up some of today's desires in order to achieve tomorrow's benefits.

The point is this: When you spend in one of these five areas, you have given up the opportunity to spend in the other areas. To say it another way, *there are no independent financial decisions.* Your personal financial priorities are a function of your goals and previous commitments. The working out of those priorities is recorded by your checkbook and/or your budget. Changing priorities is a difficult and long-term process.

THE PRIORITY TRAP

Young couples typically start out with three priorities: a home, children, and financial independence. Home prices have escalated to the point that it is very difficult for a one-wage-earner family to afford even the monthly payments, much less what is required for a down payment, closing costs, basic upkeep, insurance, and on and on. The cost to raise a child from birth through college is estimated to be $250,000. Because the moneys used to clothe, feed, and educate a child are all after-tax dollars, however, substantially more than the $250,000 must be earned in order to afford that child. And financial independence becomes harder and harder to achieve as inflation erodes the purchasing power of the dollar.

The fact is that very few young families can even dream of having a home, children, *and* financial independence; therefore, they must choose among the three. If they decide on a home as their first priority, both the husband and the wife may have to work; children may be delayed or not even planned for. If the priority is children, a home or financial independence may have to be given up; and if financial independence is chosen as the top priority, perhaps children and/or a home are not reasonable alternatives.

For example, if the family income is fixed, then when a major long-term goal—such as financial independence, buying a home, or providing for the long-term needs of children—becomes a commitment, there may not be the financial resources to fund that goal without giving up something else. Accumulating for financial independence assumes that there are dollars left over to set aside for the future. Saving for a college education assumes that there are dollars available today that can be set aside for college expenses. Saving money for a down payment once again assumes that there are extra dollars available to meet that long-term goal.

CHART 8.1
OVERVIEW OF FINANCIAL OBJECTIVES

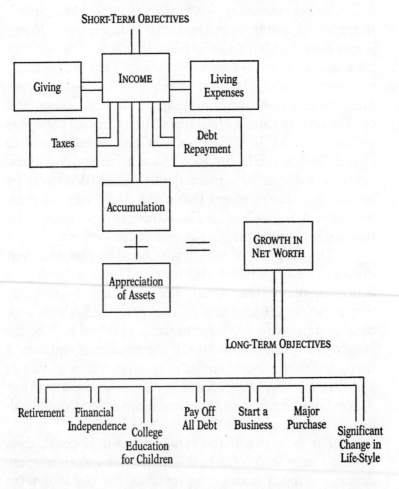

If a young family has all three goals, they may conflict to the point where one or more must be given up. It is not wrong to give up a goal, but it may be emotionally difficult to *have* to give it up. Our society, I believe, suffers under the delusion that young families can start where their parents left off. This assumption is that you can have everything right now at no long-term cost. The fact of the matter is, you can't have everything in the short term and also have everything in the long term. The chart on the facing page shows pictorially the trade-off between the short term and the long term.

Once again, unless you have unlimited resources, you cannot have everything. What you choose comes down to the bottom-line issue of priorities. What is important to you? What do you want to look back over your life, after forty years of hard work, and see that you accomplished?

Perhaps the principle of no independent financial decisions is best illustrated by Chart 8.1, Overview of Financial Objectives. When you review the chart, it is obvious that money spent in one area precludes its being spent in another area. Also, in the short term, three of the uses of money are consumptive and two are productive. Once money is spent on taxes, debt repayment, or lifestyle, it is gone forever and cannot be reused for any other purpose. On the other hand, money set aside for saving or giving is available to be used in the long-term—saving dollars to meet long-term goals and giving money to meet the eternal goals that God has for His resources.

■ ─────────────────────────────────────── ■

Unless you have unlimited resources,
you cannot have everything.

■ ─────────────────────────────────────── ■

Consumptive uses are not wrong, as is obvious by reviewing the biblical priorities outlined earlier. However, three facts are obvious when you look at the chart:

1. A dollar spent is gone forever.

2. You cannot have everything.

3. What you decide today may have an impact on all your other goals.

Before you make financial decisions, the best question to consider is always, "What is the *best use* of these resources?

Children have one consumptive use of money—spending—and they have two productive uses of money—tithing and saving. How they allocate among those three uses is also a function of their priorities. However, by the very nature of limited alternatives, they will probably save more proportionately than their parents; and they may very well give more proportionately than their parents. But how do parents train them to understand that there are no independent financial decisions?

HOW TO TRAIN CHILDREN

Giving them the *experience* of living with a limited amount of money is the key. Let us share what we have found to be effective with our children.

■ ──────────────────── ■

Once money is spent for taxes, debt repayment, or life-style, it is gone forever and cannot be reused for any other purpose.

■ ──────────────────── ■

As we stated earlier, when our children reached the age of eight or nine, they were given a clothes budget and put on a monthly clothes allowance. Judy went with them and counseled them closely the first few times they were allowed to make their decisions regarding clothes. However, after just a few times, they were given virtually total freedom to make their clothing purchases. Obviously, this meant that if they chose to spend all their money on designer jeans, they might have no new shirts; but it was our conviction that they needed to learn this principle of *no independent financial decisions.*

The only way that they can learn this is to *experience the consequences of their decisions.* We believe that it is essential for them to have the freedom to fail, and they have failed many times in their decisions. However, it has been very encouraging to see that as they got older, they had fewer and fewer failures, and a longer-term perspective became more and more important to them. It is also critical that they not be condemned or chided for their failures. Failures should be occasions for learning rather than for creating guilt. It is very easy to say to children, "Money doesn't grow on trees," but until they have to live with a limited amount of money, that truth will mean nothing to them.

A few summers ago we took our boys to Disney World for a short trip, even though we had a major family vacation planned for later in the summer. They took with them all the spending money they had been saving for the family vacation. The first day that we went to Disney World, they saw several stuffed animals and other gifts they would have liked very much to have. However, both of them realized that if they spent their money at Disney World, they would not have money to spend later on in the summer.

It was very difficult for Judy and me not to offer advice as they discussed whether to buy a stuffed Mickey Mouse; but we both felt they needed to learn that if they chose to spend the money then, they would not have it later. They agonized over their decision, but ultimately they made a good decision by spending some then and saving some for later.

It was *their* decision, and they were learning the principle that we try to teach them. Had we, as we could have easily afforded to do, given them the money to spend at Disney World, an important teaching time would have been lost.

Our society today promises, with all the power of advertising, that you can have it all. The reality is that you cannot. If you choose to consume today, it is gone forever. That's true whether you are a child or an adult. A tree cut down and used for firewood is consumed; a tree cut into lumber may be used to build a home, which has productivity for decades to come. A child who spends his money does not have it available for uses and priorities later on. An adult who does not save, or give, has no "lumber" for the future. That "lumber" may be a home, a college education, or retirement.

God has entrusted you with many valuable resources—His resources. Are you spending, saving, and giving His resources wisely? Your children are also God's valuable resources. Are you equipping them to live their lives in a manner pleasing to God, so they, in turn, can influence succeeding generations to godly living?

It is true that you only go around once in life. Are you living your life so that your grandchildren will have a godly heritage? In Colossians 1:10, Paul prays that "you may walk worthy of the Lord, fully pleasing Him." This should be your goal. Multiply your life. Teach your children to be good stewards of *all* they have; teach them to be lumber, not firewood.

Who Is Financially Mature?

One of my earliest childhood memories is of my family's garden. The company that my father worked for provided garden plots for employees, and I remember traveling with my parents to the plot, preparing the ground, sowing the seeds, tending the seedlings, and eventually harvesting the crop of tomatoes, beans, sweet corn, and cucumbers. I can still remember how good they tasted, even though I was no more than four or five years old at the time we had that garden. I also know we only reaped what we had planted. Never did we have any surprises about what grew in the garden.

The Bible has much to say about the principle of sowing and reaping. In 2 Corinthians 9:6 Paul said, "He who sows sparingly will also reap sparingly, and he who sows bountifully will also reap bountifully." (See also Gal. 6:8–9 and John 4:35–38.) There is a lot to be learned from sowing and reaping, and I want to pull one small part of that principle out in talking about the financial principle of delayed gratification.

Delayed gratification means that I give up today's desire for a future benefit. For example, I may choose to take a less expensive vacation than I really desire in order to save for future retirement. If I don't save, that benefit will not be available to me then. So my immediate desire is sacrificed in order to experience the future benefit. The problem is that this is contrary to a child's nature, to my nature, and to the world system, which teaches immediate gratification.

This principle is critical to financial success because unless you receive an inheritance, strike it rich in an investment, or otherwise have a windfall, you will not be able to have everything immediately. This can cause frustration if your perspective is totally short-term. Delayed gratification requires a long-term perspective and is the key to financial maturity. *Financial maturity* can be defined as "giving up today's desires for future benefits."

■ ─────────────────────────────── ■

Delayed gratification requires a long-term perspective and is the key to financial maturity.

■ ─────────────────────────────── ■

THREE KEY CONCEPTS

To help you understand the importance of this principle, we will illustrate three key concepts. First, we will discuss the difference between consumptive and productive uses of money. Second, we will talk about the principle of the "opportunity cost" of consumption by illustrating the "magic of compounding." Third, we will look at the concept of financial maturity in greater detail.

Productive Uses of Money

Looking again at our Overview of Financial Objectives chart (9.1), we see that only one of the five short-term uses of money provides financially to meet the long-term goals we have. These long-term financial goals are attaining financial independence, paying off debt, providing for major acquisitions such as a home, starting a business, and significant giving. Where does the money come from to meet these needs? The amount of money spent in the short term must be reduced so that funds can accumulate.

CHART 9.1
OVERVIEW OF FINANCIAL OBJECTIVES

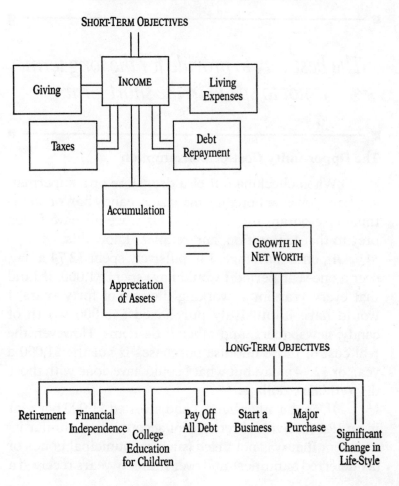

To say it another way, if the money is consumed on life-style and debt in the short term, there is no way to provide for long-term goals unless you receive an inheritance, acquire more debt, receive a higher income later on, or succeed with a get-rich-quick scheme.

The best way to provide for the long term is not to spend in the short term; making saving a little bit over a long term period a priority. Recall our illustration of a tree used for firewood. Once it has been consumed, it is no longer available for building the house or perhaps making the paper for a book, which continues to produce benefit for a long time.

The best way to provide for the long term is not to spend in the short term.

The Opportunity Cost of Consumption

When checking out of a drugstore or a supermarket, have you ever bought a magazine, candy bar, or something else on an impulse? Obviously, we all have fallen prey to that temptation, and retailers know this.

If, on the average, I impulsively spent $2.74 a day, over a one-year period I would have spent $1,000. If I did that every year for a working lifetime of forty years, I would have impulsively purchased $40,000 worth of candy, newspapers, and other little items. However, the real cost of those impulse purchases is not the $1,000 a year, or $2.74 a day, but what I could have done with those discretionary dollars.

If, on the other hand, I had invested $1,000 per year in an IRA (individual retirement account) or a similar investment that was not taxed (such as municipal bonds or tax-deferred annuities), and over the forty years received a yield of 12.5 percent compounded annually, I would have not $40,000 at age sixty-five (assuming I began this plan at age twenty-five), but $1 million. In other words, choosing to spend the $2.74 a day cost me what I *could* have earned—$1 million. This is the opportunity cost of consumption.

Another illustration is even more dramatic. The first significant purchase that most young people make is an automobile. If we assume that they pay $10,000 in cash for their first automobile rather than invest the same $10,000, what is the opportunity cost of consumption? What would the $10,000 have grown to over a forty-year period? Let's assume a 25 percent earnings rate compounded semi-annually, which historically in some mutual funds is not out of the question. The $10,000 would have grown to $75,231,000 over forty years if it were compounded at 25 percent interest, ignoring the tax consequences of that growth.

■ ──────────────────────────────── ■

A dollar spent today does not take a dollar out of the future; it takes multiple dollars out of the future.

■ ──────────────────────────────── ■

The point is this: A dollar spent today does not take a dollar out of the future; it takes multiple dollars out of the future. Or conversely; a dollar saved today puts multiple dollars in the future. To say it another way, you don't have to save $1 million to have $1 million; that is the magic of compounding.

Delayed gratification pays you back multiple dollars for a dollar, not dollar-for-dollar. That is why this principle is so critical to grasp.

Financial Maturity

We previously defined *financial maturity* as "giving up today's desires for future benefits." In the last chapter we talked about not being able to have a home, children, *and* financial independence. That may or may not be true for everyone, but it is certainly true for those who consume in the present. Many do not understand the principle of delayed gratification, and many are not willing to wait for it to take effect. However, the result is the same in both cases: no money to meet long-term goals.

The truth of financial maturity is also the truth of spiritual maturity. Christians are willing by the very act of becoming Christians to give up today's desires for future benefits. We live with the hope of eternal reward rather than succumb to the materialistic philosophy of our society or any other vain short-term philosophy.

You must train your children to be financially mature. It is essential not only for their own satisfaction and peace of mind, but also for their spiritual well-being. God will not reward those who desire, and are motivated by, instant gratification.

TEACHING CHILDREN
FINANCIAL MATURITY

Teaching children the principle of financial maturity, or delayed gratification, is something that must be caught rather than taught. So, you need to provide the environment for them to ultimately "catch" the truth of this principle.

There are several ways that this can be done. Judy and I have found that one effective way is to require them to have a savings account. A portion of all money that they receive, from whatever source, goes into a savings account. But here is a critical point: We allow them to make withdrawals from the account. They may dip into their savings for major purchases such as a dress for a special occasion, a trip, a tennis racquet, a bicycle, a stereo, or some other item they desire. They quickly learn the thrill of being able to acquire something they would really like to have by saving for it, not by receiving a handout. In other words, they learn about delayed gratification.

If we require them to make major purchases out of their savings account, they also quickly learn about limited resources. If their funds are depleted, they can't buy something they may really want. A few disappointments like that go a long way in teaching them wisdom in spending.

We have them open a savings account that pays interest, and then on a quarterly, semiannual, or annual basis, we sit down with them and show them how much interest has been earned. We explain that they did not work for that interest—they allowed the money to work for them. It is incredible how quickly they begin to understand the magic of compounding when they realize that interest earns interest, which earns interest, which earns interest, which earns interest, which earns interest, ad infinitum.

We also attempt to teach our children financial maturity by illustrating other ways to benefit from the magic of compounding. When Cynthia, our oldest, was beginning to baby-sit to earn money, I pointed out to her that if she earned $20 a week for twenty-six weeks, over a five-year period she would have earned $2,600. At that time she would be seventeen years old. If she left that $2,600 to accumulate in an account earning 12.5 percent compounded annually, until she retired at age sixty-five, forty-eight years later, her $20 a week would have grown to $741,812.98. If she chose to earn $40 a week, rather than $20 a week, for the same twenty-six week period over five years, her baby-sitting would pay off forty-eight years later to the tune of $1,483,625.95.

It was merely an illustration, but I remember it

was mind-boggling to her to realize the magic of compounding. I was quick to point out, however, that if she spent the $20 a week she earned, her real cost of spending the money was $741,812.98.

Did she learn the principle when it was illustrated in that way? I have to admit that our kids have not learned the principle totally; however, all of them can quote that $10,000 compounded at 25 percent for forty years equals $75,231,000 because I have repeated it to them many, many times.

As we've stated before, effective communication is consistent and repetitive. Children may not learn something the first time or the second, third, fourth, or even the fortieth time. But if communication is consistent and repetitive, they will eventually make what you are teaching a practice of life. Remember, also, communication is more than verbal. What does your daily life-style say to your children?

Delayed gratification may be the most difficult principle to teach your children because there is no support in our world system for it. However, it is biblical, and it is truth. It will work if they apply it. There is a caution, however, regarding this principle, and our daughter, Karen, made me vividly aware of it.

Remember communication is more than verbal. What does your daily life-style say to your children?

After perhaps the hundredth time that I had shared with the family the magic of compounding, Karen asked, "Daddy, how much is no fun compounded over forty years at 10 percent?" We all got a great laugh out of her question, but it makes a very valid point: *Money is nothing more than a resource.* In no way do I want to teach or imply that the only objective in life is to accumulate as much as possible.

Because we are stewards of God's resources, it may very well be that He would have us to spend His resources on vacations and entertainment. These could be considered frivolous unless we put them into the perspective that God meets not only the financial needs of our family, but also the emotional, social, mental, and physical needs. And money is one of the resources He uses to meet them.

Philippians 4:19 assures us that "God shall supply all [our] need according to His riches in glory by Christ Jesus." First Timothy 6:17 reminds us that God "gives us richly all things to enjoy." So we must take time to enjoy all we have.

To spend indiscriminately, with no realization of true financial cost, is to succumb to the self-defeating temptation to enjoy it while we can.

On the other hand, to spend indiscriminately, with no realization of true financial cost, is to succumb to the self-defeating temptation to enjoy it while we can. That is a deceitful philosophy and the price we pay is more than financial.

A Hated Word—*Budgeting*

Someone once asked me if I could sum up all that I knew about stewardship and money management in just a few words. After praying for wisdom and thinking about it briefly, I said, "I believe that everything I know regarding financial success can be summed up this way: 'Spend less than you earn, and do it for a long time.'"

■ ─────────────────────────────────── ■

Spend less than you earn, and do it for a long time.

■ ─────────────────────────────────── ■

Because that statement will always work, it can be called a principle. Principles will work regardless of the situation. So spending less than you earn will work regardless of your age or income level.

However, many times skills may be required to fully implement principles. Skills are tools to be learned and used in applying principles. Skills all by themselves have no meaning. The principles give them meaning.

So let's begin by looking at one financial skill that needs to be mastered in order to apply the principles previously mentioned. To refresh your memory, the four principles are these:

1. God owns it all.
2. There is always a trade-off between time-and-effort and money-and-rewards.
3. There is no such thing as an "independent" financial decision.
4. Delayed gratification is the key to financial maturity.

These four financial skills:

1. How to develop a one-year spending plan.
2. How to buy wisely.
3. How to make financial decisions.
4. How to set financial goals.

There are other financial skills, such as the skill of investing, but these four are basic for successful money management.

A budget is a short-term spending plan that includes income from all sources and preallocated uses of that income. For children, there are basically three uses: tithing, saving, and spending. For adults, there are five primary uses, as previously illustrated: tithing, paying taxes, repaying debt, spending, and saving. Within each category there may be subcategories.

BENEFITS OF BUDGETING

I remember the first time that we developed a budget. I worked on it quite a while and finally allocated our income among the five categories. I put in detailed amounts in the spending category, and one of the lifestyle, or spending, categories was "vacation and entertainment." Once the vacation budget amount had been set and put into the annual budget, I had a tremendous amount of freedom knowing what the limits were going to be. This freedom, through predetermined boundaries on spending, enabled me to spend without feeling guilty.

By going through the process of budgeting before the year began, I made several decisions prior to the fact, such as the vacation budget, clothes budget, entertainment budget, and so on. A budget tends to focus decision making on priorities.

The exercise of preparing a budget is more important, I believe, than attempting to control that budget. I am not saying that you should not control your spending; but I am saying that the *process* of preparing the budget is 60 percent to 70 percent of what it takes to live on a budget. The control aspect is mechanical.

When the budget is prepared, decisions are made, and priorities are set. You and your spouse can have unity on how you will spend your income for the next twelve months. If decisions are made in advance and priorities set in the spending plan, control is easier because you have already figured out *why* you are doing what you are doing. In addition to promoting unity, freedom, and focus on priorities, budgeting helps you to avoid debt and to spot problems before they surface.

THE FAMILY BUDGET

Chart 10.1, Living Expenses, gives some suggested budget categories you can use as a guideline in setting up your own one-year spending plan. You will notice that there are three columns: monthly, periodic, and the total annual amount. Some expenses are paid on a regular monthly basis; others occur infrequently during the year, but in a larger lump sum, for example, vacation, insurance premiums, or property taxes.

Many times in budgeting we forget those larger periodic amounts, and they are what tend to break our budget. The auto repair that we know will be needed at some point can destroy the spending plan for a particular month unless we plan for it. We recommend that these periodic expenses be estimated through this budget and the money set aside on a regular basis in a separate savings account.

Certain concepts in budgeting are important to understand. The first one is that a budget is a plan, before the fact; however, it is subject to change with new information and facts. A budget is *not* a law; it is a guideline to be followed. When a budget becomes a law, it is a taskmaster; when it is a guideline to be followed, it is a friend.

As we mentioned, it is absolutely essential to plan for the periodic and unexpected, or the surprises will always keep you behind. The only way to do this is to begin right now in saving for the periodic and unexpected. It may take a couple of years before you actually have enough set aside in savings to meet the unexpected, but it is certainly worth the price.

■ ——————————————————————————— ■

When a budget becomes a law, it is a taskmaster; when it is a guideline to be followed, it is a friend.

■ ——————————————————————————— ■

Chart 10.1, Percentage Guide for Family Income, shows some of the percentage allocations that are typical

CHART 10.1
LIVING EXPENSES

	Amount Paid Monthly	Amount Paid Other Than Monthly	Total Annual Amount
Housing			
Mortgage/Rent	$	$	$
Insurance			
Property taxes			
Electricity			
Heating			
Water			
Sanitation			
Telephone			
Cleaning			
Repairs/Maint.			
Supplies			
Other			
Total	$	$	$
Food Total	$	$	$
Clothing Total	$	$	$

	Amount Paid Monthly	Amount Paid Other Than Monthly	Total Annual Amount
Medical Expenses			
Insurance	$	$	$
Doctors			
Dentists			
Drugs			
Insurance			
Life			
Disability			
Other			
Total	$	$	$
Children			
School lunches			
Allowances			
Tuition			
Total	$	$	$

Transportation

Insurance _____ _____ _____

Gas and oil _____ _____ _____

Repairs/Maint. _____ _____ _____

Parking _____ _____ _____

Other _____ _____ _____

Total $ _____ $ _____ $ _____

Entertainment/Recreation

Eating out _____ _____ _____

Baby-sitters _____ _____ _____

Mags./Newspapers _____ _____ _____

Vacation _____ _____ _____

Clubs/Activities _____ _____ _____

Other _____ _____ _____

Total $ _____ $ _____ $ _____

Lessons _____ _____ _____

Other _____ _____ _____

Total $ _____ $ _____ $ _____

Gifts

Christmas _____ _____ _____

Birthdays _____ _____ _____

Anniversary _____ _____ _____

Other _____ _____ _____

Total $ _____ $ _____ $ _____

Miscellaneous

Toiletries _____ _____ _____

Husband: misc. _____ _____ _____

Wife: misc. _____ _____ _____

Clng/Laundry _____ _____ _____

Animal care _____ _____ _____

Beauty/Barber _____ _____ _____

Other _____ _____ _____

Other _____ _____ _____

Total $ _____ $ _____ $ _____

Total Living Expenses $ _____ $ _____ $ _____

for different income levels, assuming a family of four. Again, these numbers are guidelines rather than the law and should be used as such.

One of the most important concepts that this chart illustrates is that of *net spendable income*. The first three

CHART 10.2
PERCENTAGE GUIDE FOR FAMILY INCOME

	$20,000	$30,000	$40,000	$50,000	$60,000	$	%
Gross Income (100%)							
Less:							
Giving	10%	10%	10%	10%	10%		
Taxes and Social Security	17%	18%	19%	22%	22%		
Debt	0%	0%	0%	0%	0%		
Total Priority Expenses	27%	28%	29%	32%	32%		
Net Spendable Income	73%	72%	71%	68%	68%		
Living Expenses Housing	26%	25%	21%	20%	18%		
Food	15%	12%	9%	7%	7%		
Clothing	4%	4%	4%	3%	3%		
Transportation	10%	7%	6%	5%	5%		
Entertainment/ Recreation	4%	5%	5%	5%	5%		
Medical	2%	2%	2%	2%	2%		
Insurance	1%	2%	2%	2%	2%		
Children	2%	1%	1%	1%	1%		
Gifts	1%	1%	1%	1%	1%		
Miscellaneous	4%	4%	4%	3%	3%		
Total Living Expenses	69%	63%	55%	49%	47%		
Margin	4%	9%	16%	18%	21%		

NOTE: All percentages are of gross income.
Assumptions:
1. Figures are based on a family of four.
2. The tax deductions are giving, interest on home mortgage, and state and property taxes.
3. Home is owned.
4. There is no debt other than home mortgage.
5. All Social Security withholdings are from one wage earner.
6. Margin can be used for other expenses (private education, savings, etc.)

priority uses of funds are the tithe, taxes, and debt repayment. The amount of income that can be used for living expenses is the net spendable amount *after* the tithe, taxes, and debt have been set aside. Therefore, every dollar of income is *not* totally available to spend. Many families get out of control financially because they assume that when a raise occurs, or extra income is available, it is totally available to spend. But if you tithe, and you certainly have to pay taxes on all income, at best only a percentage of the increased income is available to spend on your life-style.

Once a budget has been set, you will need to have some form of control on spending to ensure that the amounts spent for each category fall within the budget limits. You can do this by summarizing, on a regular basis, the amounts spent for each budget category and comparing them against the plan. An actual control process for parents is described in detail in *Master Your Money*, and in chapter 5 of this book for children.

■ —————————————————————————— ■

Every dollar of income is not *totally available to spend.*

■ —————————————————————————— ■

A CHILD'S BUDGET

Obviously, a child's budget in no way needs to be as detailed as your family's budget. However, the basic concepts of budgeting are still applicable.

Rule 1 in helping your child to budget is to keep it simple, using just a few budget categories. The number of categories will increase as the child becomes older. For example, an eight-year-old may have just four categories to budget: tithing, saving, spending, and purchasing clothes. In the teen years, other categories will be added such as sports, music lessons, clothes (which could have sub-categories), and car expenses. By the time a child reaches college age, additional categories may be added, such as college tuition, books, entertainment, food, and housing allowance.

Rule 2 is to let the budget be the child's, not yours. Let the child set the categories and name them; don't dictate categories *you* think are important. We have found that the process of helping our children budget is not a lengthy process after the first time. It is as simple as sitting down with each of them, taking out a sheet of paper, and helping them decide how much they are going to spend on a weekly, monthly, and annual basis for all the categories they have responsibility for. These amounts can then be summarized into a few budget categories, but the budget itself is nothing more than a sheet of paper with the planned expenses on it. Worksheets to help you in this process appear in chapter 5.

Rule 3 is to recognize that each child is unique in terms of age and needs. Therefore, one budget will not necessarily work for each of your children. Some will spend more on clothes or makeup than sports equipment. Some will choose to spend more on gifts or entertainment than others. What is important is that you and each child jointly set a budget for a year so that decisions are premade and priorities are set.

We have found that a major variable in the budget is the age of the child. Needs change dramatically over a relatively short period of time. For example, the clothing budget that was set at the beginning of the year for the twelve-year-old means nothing if he grows six inches that year. So you need to be flexible. Remember, a budget is not a law; it is a guide to achieving a spending pattern in accordance with preset priorities. It is a boundary within which there is great freedom to operate.

A budget is not a law; it is a guide to achieving a spending pattern in accordance with preset priorities.

CONCLUSION

Mention the word *budget* and almost invariably people think about lack of freedom, constraints, inflexibility, rigidity, guilt, and other negative images. In reality, making a budget is the same as taking a trip with a pre-planned route. When you get to an intersection, you know which way to go. Rather than create rigidity, a budget brings freedom. It lessens confusion, fear, and frustration.

Living without a short-term spending plan will inevitably cause feelings of fear, frustration, confusion and, in a marriage relationship, conflict. If lack of planning evokes these emotions in adults, imagine the effect it can have on a child trying to learn how to handle money.

Two years spent in strict budgeting can prepare your children for a lifetime of financial freedom.

Give your children financial freedom by paying the price of teaching them the skill of budgeting. When they learn this skill and apply it, it will become a habit. Two years spent in strict budgeting can prepare your children for a lifetime of financial freedom.

Getting Money the Easy Way

T he skill of buying wisely can be explained as buying what is *needed* at the *best* price. The best price is not necessarily the lowest price, however. For example, if you spend $15 for a dress that fades after one washing and therefore is not usable again, the cost per wearing is $15. On the other hand, if you spend $75 for another dress that can be worn for several years, the cost per use drops dramatically. So, wise buying is buying what you need at the best price with the longest-range perspective possible.

Another factor to consider when evaluating what to buy is the cost of inconvenience. For example, buying a used car for $500 that needs to be taken to the repair shop on a weekly basis probably costs more in terms of inconvenience and repairs than buying another used car for $3,000, $4,000 or even $5,000.

THE VALUE OF BUYING WISELY

Ben Franklin said, "A penny saved is a penny earned," but that is not really true, as we learned in chapter 9. A penny saved may be, over time, a dollar earned rather than a penny earned. The point, however, is that to save a penny by not spending it is the quickest way to have *discretionary dollars*. Discretionary dollars are those that can be used to meet long-term goals and objectives. If you are faithful in buying what is needed at the best price, taking into account the cost per use, the cost of inconvenience, and the cost of repairs, these decisions over time will have a compounding effect. They will then provide the discretionary cash to meet some of your long-term goals and objectives.

THE PRIMARY PROBLEM

The primary problem associated with buying wisely is that all of us are impulse buyers, at least to some extent. We've already discussed how costly it can be in the long run to buy that candy bar or magazine at the checkout counter. We seldom go to the grocery store strictly to buy a candy bar or a magazine, yet we often come home with one of those impulse purchases.

■ ─────────────────────────────────── ■

The more credit cards we have, the more we tend to purchase.

■ ─────────────────────────────────── ■

Credit card companies know that we are impulse purchasers. They know that putting a new credit card in our hands results in more impulse purchases. We do not stop using our other credit cards just because we have a new one. The more credit cards we have, the more we tend to purchase, regardless of whether we can really afford it or not. Many times I've been in line at a store and observed people flipping through credit cards, trying to decide which ones still have credit available on them.

As mentioned earlier, we have redefined "being able to afford it" as "being able to afford the payments." Credit card companies estimate that using credit cards will result in our spending 34 percent more than if we used cash.

Judy and I did not really believe that statistic until several years ago when we went on a straight cash budget for one year and used cash for every purchase. Because we were able to account for our expenses very accurately, we were able to measure that our living expenses dropped by more than 30 percent just by using cash rather than credit cards. We were astounded by those results.

■ ─────────────────────────────── ■

Almost all financial scams ... are structured so that they require an immediate decision.

■ ─────────────────────────────── ■

However, not only minor purchases are bought on an impulse. Many decisions about major purchases—cars, boats, watches, suits, vacations, and investments—are typically made on an impulse. Having a budget will help avoid that problem, but learning and practicing the skill of wise buying will help avoid it too.

Almost all financial scams—lotteries, "free" weekends, and vacations—are structured so that they require an immediate decision.

THE SOLUTION

We have four rules to help you avoid making impulse purchases:

Rule 1. *Never* use credit or credit cards for an impulse purchase.

Rule 2. When confronted with the opportunity to make an impulse purchase, discipline yourself to wait at least one week before spending the money.

Rule 3. Before making the impulse decision, share your decision and your decision-making process with at least one another person.

Rule 4. For the really serious impulse buyers, find an accountability partner with whom you must share every financial decision. Let that person hold you accountable to the commitment not to make impulse purchases.

During lunch one Sunday, we asked our children for their ideas on how to buy wisely. We offered no insight or encouragement; we merely recorded what they had to say. Here is what they have learned through experience and guidance:

- Watch for sales.
- Buy quality.
- Before you go shopping, set a dollar limit on what you will spend, and take only that amount with you.
- Don't browse, contrary to the popular motto, "Shop 'til you drop."
- Never take credit cards on a shopping trip.
- Wait two days on an impulse purchase.
- Plan what you will buy.
- Live by your budget.
- Think about the purchase.
- When buying clothes, (a) make a list of what you have before going shopping—in other words, take an inventory; (b) decide what will go with the rest of your wardrobe and shop for specifics; and (c) don't just shop for whatever catches your eye.
- Always get advice from brothers or sisters or parents before buying.

These were their ideas, and quite frankly, when I read through the list, I realized how often I don't follow these rules. Children really are both wise and teachable.

HOW TO TEACH YOUR CHILDREN
WISE BUYING

Probably the best way to teach your children wise buying is to take them with you when you are shopping and let them share in your decision-making process. Then they will understand why you do what you do. Next, give them counsel and the freedom to fail in making their own buying decisions.

I remember when Karen decided that she wanted to shop for clothing at a major department store instead of at the discount store her mother preferred. Judy felt that Karen would be better off at the discount store because her money would go further. However, she gave Karen the right to choose where she wanted to shop for clothes.

Karen had been counseled on what to look for in making purchases, so she always went to the department store with a specific idea or a list in mind as to what she wanted to buy. Invariably, she has been able to buy the clothing she desired because she knew specifically what she wanted. She also gave up having more of certain clothes in order to buy exactly what she wanted in a name brand line of clothing. This is okay with us. It is important that she is willing to wear whatever she buys; the cost per wearing is more important, we believe, than the actual cost.

Another way that children can be taught how to buy wisely is to participate in the repairs and maintenance of the home. They learn these necessary skills, as well as the costs of not doing something right the first time or the savings which result from do-it-yourself projects. They can help with painting, fixing plumbing problems, repairing light fixtures, remodeling a room, and on and on, limited only by the skill of the parent who is the teacher.

It is difficult at best to practice the skill of buying wisely in our affluent society. As we have observed, that skill is not even honored today. If anything, people who have the discipline, desire, and skill of buying wisely are scorned in our society. Therefore, parents need patience and time to teach your children how to buy wisely. You are the role models, and you will have to practice this skill before you can ever hope to teach it to your children.

Decision Making

Our children often ask us to make decisions for them. "Should I buy these shoes?" "Should I go to the mall with Kim?" "What should I do?" "How do I know?" The way we answer these questions conveys to our children something about values, opinions, and priorities. Helping them learn to make sound decisions now will affect how they cope in their adult lives.

■ ───────────────────────────────── ■

Failing to teach your children how to make decisions robs them of a vital skill for the process of living.

■ ───────────────────────────────── ■

Decision making involves choosing from among various alternatives; and because it does, it is always future-related. Failing to teach your children how to make decisions robs them of a vital skill for the process of living. On a daily basis everyone is confronted with the need for decision making, some more important than others.

An implicit assumption in decision making is that once a choice has been made and acted on, various personal objectives and priorities will be satisfied. For example, our two boys once decided that they had saved enough money to buy the bicycles they wanted. We took them to the bicycle shop, and each of them made a decision based on cost, color, and style. When they had made their decisions, they had satisfied *their* objectives of cost, color, and style. However, they did not buy the same bicycle because they had different priorities regarding color and style.

■ ──────────────────────────────────── ■

Every decision required making a choice from among many alternatives, and it satisfied the objectives and priorities of the person or persons making it.

■ ──────────────────────────────────── ■

One of our sons asked many, many questions about our opinions, and then he chose a bicycle that neither Judy nor I would have chosen. That was okay, though, because *his* objectives and priorities needed to be met, not ours. What we tried to do in answering his questions was to point him back to evaluating his real objectives and priorities. The boys were pleased with their final decisions, not because of the bicycles per se, but because their objectives and priorities had been met.

Some of the major decisions we have made through the years as a family involved summer jobs, college choices, summer school, where to go on vacation, what house to purchase, what clothes to buy, the bicycles, and more. Every decision required making a choice from among many alternatives, and it satisfied the objectives and priorities of the person or persons making it.

DECISION-MAKING IS A SKILL

I was thirty-five years old when someone finally introduced me to the process of decision making by Colonel Nimrod McNair, a good friend. Even though I had received both B.A. and M.B.A. degrees, spent between forty and eighty hours per year in professional development training, started and run my own business, and made two major career changes, no one had ever taught me a process of decision making. I first learned about the process when I joined Leadership Dynamics International, an organization formed specifically to teach this skill.

Having practiced the skill of decision making many times, I have observed that many persons instinctively make good decisions, but few understand the process they go through in making these decisions. Knowing the process gives freedom and security. It provides a means for properly evaluating a decision without overlooking other things that need to be considered.

Many years ago in a restaurant one day, Judy and I went through the decision-making process. The decision we made (and wrote down on the back of a napkin) led us into the business and ministry we now have. There has never been a question since then that we are where God would have us to be. Because of the process we went through, it was absolutely clear what career I should be involved in for the rest of my life.

Training children to make decisions is equipping them to live successfully. The skill of decision making affects all areas of life, but it is more frequently used in making financial decisions than in other types of decisions.

DECISION MAKING INVOLVES A PROCESS

Saying that decision making involves a *process* means that there is a sequence of steps to go through to arrive at the result, which is a decision. However, before you can get into the process, you must avoid three common traps that Bruce Cook of Leadership Dynamics has identified and named: the binary trap, the intuitive trap, and the voting trap.

■ ───────────────────────────── ■

Training children to make decisions is equipping them to live successfully.

■ ───────────────────────────── ■

The *binary trap* is one we face daily when the decision comes phrased as, Should I do this or not? Should I buy this car or not? Should I buy this house or not? Should I buy this sweater or not? Should I go to this college or not? Should I choose this job or not?

■ ───────────────────────────── ■

A decision can never be any better than the alternatives recognized and evaluated.

■ ───────────────────────────── ■

As you can see, the binary trap has only two alternatives—to do something or not to do it. Here is the key point: A decision can never be any better than the alternatives recognized and evaluated; therefore, if you leave yourself with only two alternatives, your decision can never be any better than these two choices. When you consider only two, you may not consider another idea that might prove the best alternative.

The way to get out of the binary trap is to ask three questions:

1. What am I really trying to accomplish by making this decision?

2. What is the best ———? It could be the best use of funds, the best use of time, the best use of talent, the best whatever. By asking this question, you open up the possibility of many *other* alternatives.

3. Are there any other alternatives? If the answer is yes (in almost every case there are alternatives), obviously your decision will be better because you have considered those alternatives also.

The second trap that everyone falls into at one time or another is the *intuitive trap*. This means that you make a decision on the basis of how you "feel" about it. If you ask others why they make a particular decision almost invariably they will say, "I feel good about this decision," "I felt it was the right decision," or "It seemed to be the right decision." In every case they intuitively made the decision.

■ —————————————————————————— ■

Every decision should be made to fulfill prioritized objectives, not feelings.

■ —————————————————————————— ■

Consider this: Every decision should be made to fulfill or prioritize objectives, not feelings. Feelings may be indicators of the objectives, but they are not the objectives.

You get out of the intuitive trap by asking two questions:

1. What are the objectives I am trying to accomplish?

2. Does each objective have the same priority? Are they all of equal importance to me?

The third trap is the *voting trap*. You simply make a decision based on a survey of your friends. This process assumes that your advisers have the same goals and priorities you do, and that is why it is a trap. They won't!

Seeking counsel is certainly advisable. Proverbs 11:14 cautions: "Where there is no counsel, the people fall; / But in the multitude of counselors there is safety." But that counsel should tell you about the validity of *your* goals and objectives; it should not take the form of a gathering of opinions with the majority ruling.

You get out of the voting trap by asking this question: Is this my decision or the collective decision of my friends and counselors?

Now you are ready to get into the actual decision-making process. This process includes six steps in sequence as follows:

1. *Write out or verbalize the actual decision to be made.* For example, I must choose where to live; I must choose the best transportation to and from work; I must choose how to earn an income to support my family.

2. *List the objectives,* such as minimize cost, maximize convenience, and so on.

3. *Prioritize the objectives.* Not every objective will have the same priority. Some will be "must" priorities; the others will vary in importance. Give each objective a number valued from one to five, with five being absolutely essential and one being an optional objective.

4. *List all possible alternatives.* After you have

looked at your objectives and priorities, ask yourself if there are any "creative alternatives." This will help you make sure you have included all the possibilities. Your decision can be no better than your best alternative.

5. *Evaluate the alternatives in light of the objectives.* For example, if I am choosing what transportation to use to commute to work, one of the alternatives may be a new car; but one of the objectives may be for the cost to be less than two thousand dollars. This means that the objective for that alternative makes the choice a zero priority. Remember, every decision is made to accomplish certain objectives, not just to get the alternative. The alternative is only good if it meets the objectives.

6. *Choose the alternative that best meets the objectives and priorities.* This is done by adding up the "points" the alternatives have after evaluating them in light of the objectives.

This process can be expanded and made more formal than what is outlined here. However, just thinking through the steps and making a decision in an orderly and objective manner will allow you to make better decisions. You will remember what you are actually doing, which is meeting objectives and priorities, not "alternative jumping."

When the boys purchased their bicycles, they did not write out their objectives and priorities; however, they followed this process mentally. Judy and I had to continually remind ourselves that *their* objectives and priorities, not ours, needed to be met. Therefore, when they asked for advice, we avoided giving our opinion by asking them "why" questions. Why do you like this style? color? size? and so forth.

When our second daughter Denise made her college decision, we evaluated several colleges over a period of a year. In this particular case, we formalized the process by writing out the decision to be made. We looked at the objectives; we prioritized the objectives; we listed all the possible alternatives; and we evaluated those alternatives in light of the objectives.

She made the decision to attend a large university; then she was offered a basketball scholarship to a small college. When she was offered this alternative, all of a sudden her real objectives and priorities came clearly into focus. She realized that one very important priority was to be able to play college basketball. She had never considered this as an option and, therefore, had never focused on it as a high priority. When this alternative became available, we went through the process again, as follows:

CHART 12.1
DECISION: CHOOSE A COLLEGE (1)

OBJECTIVES (2)	PRIORITIES (3)	ALTERNATIVES (4)			
		College A	College B	College C	
Location—within 2 hours of Atlanta	2	2	2	0	(5)
Size—small to medium	1	1	1	1	
Variety of academic options	3	3	0	0	
Cost—less than $8,000 per year	3	3	0	3	
Opportunity to play basketball	5	0	0	5	
Opportunity for Christian fellowship	4	4	4	4	
Total	18	13	7	13	← (6)

1. Define the decision to be made.
2. List the objectives.
3. Prioritize the objectives (score from 1 to 5, with 5 being absolutely essential and 1 being an optional objective).
4. List all the alternatives.
5. Score the alternatives by evaluating whether or not the alternative meets the objective (column 2). If yes, give it the priority score (column 3). If no, give it a zero.
6. Total the score for each alternative.

When we completed this decision-making chart, College A, her original choice, and College C, the small college, came out with the same score. However, it was obvious to her and to us that the objective of playing basketball was an overriding priority. The choice was clear.

The process forced her to focus on objectives and

priorities rather than alternatives. The decision allowed her to meet her prioritized objectives. Normally, people make this type of decision based on an intuitive "feel" about the alternative under consideration, not on a formal process.

It was interesting to note that her priorities were substantially different from ours and from her sister's, who had gone through the process a year earlier. This is what decision making is all about. It is meeting personal objectives and priorities.

HOW TO TEACH

There are two types of decisions, each of which requires a different teaching process. *Short-term*, relatively unimportant, *decisions* will be encountered on a daily basis. *Major decisions*, such as those involving college, career, or a spouse, may be once-in-a-lifetime decisions; the process involving them should be much more formal.

We believe three things are important for us to remember in teaching our children how to make the short-term, relatively minor decisions. First we want to continually point them toward their real objectives and priorities. We try not to let them use the phrases, "I think" or "I feel." When they use those words, we ask, "Why do you think or feel that way?" That makes them focus on the *real* objectives and helps them stay out of the intuitive trap.

Second, we continually ask them, "Are there any other alternatives?" In both cases, we help them to avoid the binary and the intuitive traps, and to focus on a clear definition of their objectives and priorities.

Third, after the decision is made, we try to give them feedback by asking questions such as, "Did it really accomplish your objectives?" "Do you still like it?"; "Why?" or "Why not?"; "Would another alternative have been better?"; "Why didn't it come to mind?"; and so forth. These questions, as a part of the teaching process, get them to think through other alternatives, objectives, and priorities. They remind the children to gather facts and to ask themselves, What am I really trying to accomplish in making this decision?

■ ─────────────────────────────── ■

We have found that participating with our children in the major decisions is an important step in teaching them the process.

■ ─────────────────────────────── ■

The major decisions can be, and should be, much more formalized. In the major decisions in our family—college, church, home, car—we put the process down on paper for consideration, revision, and future reference. We actually state the decision to be made, list the objectives, prioritize those objectives, list our alternatives, and then record what decision was made.

After formalizing the process and making the decision, we add a last step; we evaluate the risk. We ask three questions:

1. What is the worst thing that can happen if we make this decision?

2. How likely is it to occur?

3. Are we willing to live with that risk?

If the answer to the last question is no, then we have not chosen the best alternative.

We have found that participating with our children in the major decisions is an important step in teaching them the process. We believe that our kids are leaving home with an understanding of how to apply the skill of decision making. Whether or not they choose to use it is, of course, up to them, but they have been taught a process with a sound basis, rather than an intuitive process for making decisions.

CONCLUSION

A key principle of decision making is that the longer term the perspective, the better the decision that is likely to be made today. Teach your children to think about long-term goals and make their decision by choosing the alternative that will best accomplish these goals. Their choice will thus be much more significant than if they focused only on satisfying short-term objectives. This is consistent with God's Word, which teaches a long-term perspective.

■───────────────────────────────────────■

The longer term the perspective, the better the decision that is likely to be made today.

■───────────────────────────────────────■

Another truth to teach your children is this: Wisdom comes from God. James 1:5 states, "If any of you lacks wisdom, let him ask of God, who gives to all liberally and without reproach, and it will be given to him." Wisdom from God is necessary for each step of the process, not just at the beginning or the end. His wisdom is required to know the real decision, the real objectives, the real priorities in life, and the available alternatives. Prayerful deliberation is essential to make the process work.

One aspect of teaching your children decision making may be particularly difficult for you. You must stop making their decisions for them! Give them the opportunity to make their own decisions. Give them the freedom to fail. Give them the freedom to express their priorities and objectives. Give them the freedom to learn while you are there to help and counsel them.

Obviously, you should be giving them counsel, but the counsel should be how to go through the process and how to stay in the process, not which decision to make. They will learn this skill only as they follow the process frequently. However, as with the other skills we have discussed, it is a life this skill will last them a lifetime.

Two books are particularly helpful. One is *Decision Making and the Will of God*, written by Gary Friesen and J. Robin Maxon (Multnomah Press) and the other is *Faith Planning*, written by Bruce Cook (Victor Books).

Our challenge to you is to help your children master the art of good decision making. First, allow them to make their own decisions; stop doing it for them. Second, begin using a formalized process of decision making for your own decisions. Third, teach that process to your children. Soon you'll have better understanding of—and confidence in—the decisions you and your children make.

Goal Setting

I n our family we have these sayings, "If you aim at nothing, you'll hit it every time," and "If you don't know where you're going, any road will get you there." The point is that if you have no goals, you will never know when you have arrived or how best to get where you want to be.

Many couples are driven to achieve something called financial independence. However, they have never defined what financial independence means; consequently, they will never know when they have arrived at that point nor will they know how to get there. They will spend their lives on a treadmill trying to obtain more and more and more.

Many people have arrived, but they do not know it. Like the joke about pitcher for the Atlanta Braves baseball team who drove around the perimeter of Atlanta three times and missed his first game because he did not know where to get off, many people do not get off, even though they are already where they want to be financially.

Having well-defined goals provides both direction and motivation. When I went to Indiana University in the early 1960s, I had only one goal in mind, and that was to have a good time. I did have a good time. In fact, I had such a good time that my grades were never very good until I met Judy, set the goal to become a CPA, and got married. Then my grades went from average to very good. During the interviewing process, recruiters used to ask me what happened. The answer was very simple. I determined what I wanted to do, set a goal and, consequently, had the motivation to achieve that goal.

Having well-defined goals provides both direction and motivation.

Because goals are such powerful motivators, it is incredibly important to set the *right* goals. For the Christian, goals are implicit statements of God's will because they are always future-oriented. You could restate a goal in these terms: I believe this is what God wants me to accomplish some time in the future.

The *real* goals in life are not financial, but finances may be the way to achieve the goals. For example, Judy and I have the goal of providing a place for our children to bring their friends. We also want to provide a home that will enable us to have guests live with us. We have had guests live with us for varying lengths of time. Money is the resource that allows us to accomplish the goal; but the goal is not money alone. Therefore, when we set financial goals, they will help us meet the *real* goals and objectives of life.

GOALS DEFINED

A goal is a *measurable* objective toward which you are moving. The fact that you can measure it means you will always know when you have achieved the goal. A purpose statement, on the other hand, is not necessarily measurable. For example, I have as a purpose to be a good father, and Judy and I desire to be good parents. Neither is measurable, however. On the other hand, I have a goal to spend fifteen minutes each day with each child, which is a goal that will help me to accomplish the real purpose. So when we talk about goals, we are talking about something measurable.

A goal is a measurable *objective toward which you are moving.*

Goal setting is not the same as decision making. Decision making requires action now and involves a choice among alternatives. Goal setting is future oriented and has a specific objective in mind.

GOAL SETTING IS A SKILL

Like decision making, goal setting is a skill that must be practiced. Goals will change over time due to changing circumstances, priorities, and desires. Therefore, it is important to recognize that you will be resetting your goals throughout your life on a fairly frequent basis. So, how do you set those goals?

The beginning point is spending time with God. Psalm 37:4 states, "Delight yourself also in the LORD, / And He shall give you the desires of your heart." This means that as you spend time with Him, He will work in your heart to bring to the surface the desires He wants you to have.

Spend time alone with God on a daily basis. As you do, record in a journal what your heart seems to be saying or what you seem to be hearing from Him. Judy and I have found over time that God affirms the desires of our hearts; and as we record what He brings to our minds, our goals tend to become focused.

You should consider these two questions after spending time with Him: What are the goals that God would have me to set? Are they measurable? Then record the goals in a journal or notebook so that you can refer to them and see how you are doing. Remember, goals are the specific steps by which you accomplish the purposes of your life.

When you are setting goals, you are limited by your own creativity, wisdom, and knowledge if you do not spend time with God. In no way can your abilities compare with the wisdom, knowledge, power, creativity, and transcendence of the Creator God of the universe.

■ ─────────────────────────────── ■

Goals are the specific steps by which you accomplish the purposes of your life.

■ ─────────────────────────────── ■

Over time, your goals will change due to many factors, so the process must be a continuous one. As you continually spend time with God, He will give you the desires of your heart. You will define and redefine the goals that will enable you to accomplish these desires. You will be motivated and encouraged by knowing what your goals are in relation to God's best for your life.

Life is a process, and one of the things that gives it meaning and fulfillment is the accomplishment of God-given goals. In his book *Success, Motivation and the Scrip-*

tures William H. Cook defines *success* as "the continued achievement of God-given goals." If you are continually achieving the goals that God has given you, then when you stand before Him, you will stand before Him as a "success."

CHART 13.1

EXAMPLES OF GOAL SETTING BY PARENTS

STEP	PARENTS' GOALS		
	Example #1	Example #2	Example #3
1	Spend time with God.	Spend time with God.	Spend time with God.
2	Desire to become more physically fit.	Desire to practice hospitality.	Desire to increase tithing.
3	Lose weight.	Invite couples over.	Begin tithing.
4	Lose eight pounds by Dec. 1	Have two couples over next month.	Give 10% of gross income weekly.
5	Post goal on 3″x5″ card on my mirror.	Put times on calendar.	Put Post-it note in checkbook as reminder of my objective.
6	No more desserts. Keep track of calories. Weigh in daily and record weight.	Decide on couples to invite. Make telephone calls.	Determine income each week; multiply by 10 percent; write a check.
7	Review progress daily.	Confirm that goal has been accomplished within one week.	Keep track of income and expense on a monthly basis, noting the changes that occur from the original plan.

We follow a seven-step process in setting goals:

Step 1: Spend time with God.
Step 2: Write general impressions and desires that come from that time with God in a journal.
Step 3: Record a specific goal.

Step 4: Make the goal measurable.
Step 5: Make the measurable goal visible.
Step 6: Outline the action steps (subgoals).
Step 7: Review.

Charts 13.1–13.2, Examples of Goal Setting by Parents and Examples of Goal Setting by Children, illustrate how the process has worked for us.

CHART 13.2
EXAMPLES OF GOAL SETTING BY CHILDREN

STEP	CHILDREN'S GOALS		
	Example #1	Example #2	Example #3
1	Spend time with God.	Spend time with God.	Spend time with God.
2	Desire to be liked.	Desire for a bicycle.	Do better in school.
3	Have more friends.	Buy bicycle.	Improve grades.
4	Make two new friends by end of school year.	Buy bicycle by Mar. 1	Have all *A*'s and *B*'s for at least one grading period.
5	Post goal on 3"x5" card on my mirror.	Cut out picture of bicycle and put over my bed.	Post my grades over my desk.
6	Invite two kids over per month to spend night; become involved in a club; go to youth meetings at church each week.	Save $2 per week; save all gift money from birthday and Christmas; visit stores to price bicycles; watch for ads in newspaper.	Talk to teachers to get counsel as to help needed; develop study plan; study one more hour at school; study one hour per night and 3 hours per weekend; have parents review work.
7	Talk to my parents about the friends I am meeting.	Pray regularly for the goal.	Determine at end of each quarter if goal is reached.

HOW TO TEACH YOUR CHILDREN TO SET GOALS

Goal setting is important, but rarely is it urgent. I doubt that your child will come to you and say, "Please help me set some goals." Unlike decision making that confronts you with the necessity of choosing among alternatives on a daily basis, there is almost no pressure to set goals.

Because of this we have found that it is necessary to set aside a specific time for goal setting. The best time we have found to do this is on each child's birthday each year, beginning at age eight. As mentioned earlier, on that day, we take the child out for a special dinner, just the three of us. During the course of the dinner, we review what goals were set a year ago, whether or not they have been accomplished, and then talk about the goals the child would like to set for the next year. We record those goals in a book that has several pages reserved for each child. This process really helps the children focus on the activities they want to participate in and how God would have them use their time and talents.

In some cases, we will set goals during the year and post them on the refrigerator so that they can be seen on a regular basis. An example would be practicing a sport so many minutes a day, reading a certain amount of time per week, or getting specific grades in the next grading period in a difficult subject. In my case, it may be losing a certain number of pounds over the next thirty days or jogging so many minutes per day.

We make sure that the goal is measurable. It must be in front of us so that we are continually ordering our time and financial resources to accomplish it. And it must be attainable. For example, the goal to shoot twelve thousand free throws per day, seven days a week, is not realistic. Allowing a child to set this type of goal will only cause frustration.

Three principles need to be applied in teaching your children goal setting. First of all, there must be periodic review of the goals; otherwise, they are forgotten, or accomplishing them provides no reward because they are not reviewed. Second, if a goal is to be motivational, it must be recorded where you can see it on a regular basis.

Third, the goal must be measurable so that you know when it has been accomplished.

WHAT GOALS TO SET

The actual goals you and your child set are not nearly as important as the *process* of goal setting for children. We encourage our children to set goals in almost any area of life. Making friends, achieving grades, saving a certain amount, tithing, making major purchases, and being disciplined in life are areas in which our children have set goals. We encourage them to set goals; we help them set goals; and we review with them the successes and failures in achieving goals.

■ ──────────────────────────── ■

Goals help to raise the level of achievement and accomplishment.

■ ──────────────────────────── ■

One of the worst things that I can imagine is to raise our children without helping them understand their purpose in life. Having goals helps them focus on the purposes of life. How sad for individuals to reach the end of life and see how little they have accomplished. Goals help to raise the level of achievement and accomplishment.

■ ──────────────────────────── ■

Take time to set goals with your children.

■ ──────────────────────────── ■

Take time to set goals with your children. They enjoy it, they do it quite easily, and they are motivated by achieving them. It is also motivational to you as parents as you watch your children develop the maturity and independence of knowing where they are going and why.

PARENTS' FINANCIAL GOALS

Long-term goals are achieved by planning for them in the present. That means you will have to give up certain expenditures now in order to accumulate for the long term. Therefore, a complete set of financial goals would include a one-year spending plan and the long-term goals quantified by amounts and dates.

As parents, we may have seven major long-term desires, each of which can be translated into a financial goal. These are the following:

	Amount Needed	Date Needed
1. Retirement.	$_____	_____
2. Financial independence.	$_____	_____
3. College education for children.	$_____	_____
4. Pay off all debt.	$_____	_____
5. Start a business.	$_____	_____
6. A major purchase.	$_____	_____
7. A significant change in life-style.	$_____	_____

These will become goals when a date and a dollar amount have been set for them.

We encourage you, as a couple, to sit down and prayerfully set your long-term financial goals. A husband and wife must have unity in their financial goals. If they do not, there will invariably be conflict over which goals take priority. As you are setting goals as a couple, share the process with your children. Help them develop their own goals, but remember, let them find their own way. Don't be swayed into setting goals for them.

■ ———————————————————————————————————— ■

Goal setting can be a tremendous communication tool for the entire family. It helps you to focus on where you will be spending your time and dollar resources.

■ ———————————————————————————————————— ■

Goal setting can be a tremendous communication tool for the entire family. It helps you to focus on where you will be spending your time and dollar resources, and it gives your family a sense of purpose and direction.

Part 4

Additional Helps

14

But What About...?

A t this point, if you were to reflect on what has been covered so far, I am sure you could think of other money management topics that may cause you some concern. What about peer pressure, checking accounts, credit cards, cars, college education costs, loans to married children, or homes for married children? In this chapter we will discuss various issues and some ways to deal with them.

PEER PRESSURE

Earlier, we used the illustration of one of our daughters who preferred to shop at a department store rather than at a discount store for her clothes. The envelope system gives her the freedom to shop where she wants, but she must make some priority decisions in order to do that.

A close friend's teenage daughter continually wanted to have the types and styles of clothes that her friends had. She would buy something and wear it to school, but if she did not get approval from her peer group, she would never wear it again. Her behavior was creating a tremendous amount of conflict in the family because they were unable to financially provide for her endless whims and desires.

When this couple learned of the envelope system and instituted it in the family, the problem immediately went away. The daughter had *her* choice of spending *her* money on *her* clothes in any way she desired. Obviously, with a limited supply of money, she was stuck with the outfit she chose. She had no alternative but to continue to wear it, whether or not her peer group approved.

■ ──────────────────────────────── ■

> ## *Peer pressure is not a money issue; it is a self-worth issue.*

■ ──────────────────────────────── ■

This couple learned the truth that peer pressure is not a money issue; it is a self-worth issue. During the teen years peer pressure is tremendous—not because money is the goal, but because acceptance and self-worth are the goals.

Peer pressure intensifies the need for positive self-worth. With my friend's daughter, the envelope system helped identify the issue, which was self-worth, not money.

Our children certainly experience peer pressure, but by being on the envelope system of money management, they do not have to deal with peer pressure as a money issue. If they desire more clothes or different bicycles that are above and beyond their budget, the answer is simple—they can work for what they want. Very quickly they decide whether the acceptance by their peer group is as important as the time required to work to provide what the peer group says they have to have. This is obviously the same problem that we, as parents, face, and it is what our parents called "keeping up with the Joneses."

CHECKING ACCOUNTS

When I counseled one couple regarding their financial situation, the wife explained that keeping a checking account was very simple. She faithfully recorded her checks as she wrote them, and whenever she ran out of money, she used a "neat" column in her check register called "deposit." If she ran low on money, she merely added another one thousand dollars to the deposit column. However, she actually deposited nothing in the account. Upon hearing this, her husband was shocked, to say the least. But he learned why they were continually overdrawn at the bank when they had positive balances on their check registers.

■ ─────────────────────────────── ■

Balancing and maintaining a checkbook is a skill that children absolutely must have by the time they leave home.

■ ─────────────────────────────── ■

Many adults do not know how to maintain a checking account. I am always surprised to discover how many people *never* reconcile their checkbook with their bank statement; some do not know that it *is possible* to balance with the bank statement. It is no wonder that, when I talk to these people about budgeting, they have no idea where to begin. Balancing and maintaining a checkbook are skills that children absolutely must have by the time they leave home. Because children typically cannot cash checks until they have a driver's license, it is impractical for them to open a checking account until age sixteen. At that time we have opened checking accounts for each of our children and have spent some time in teaching them to balance their account on a monthly basis.

Though difficult at first, once they learn how to balance the account, they will never have to learn it again. This skill is one that both boys and girls need to know.

If you are not balancing your checkbook on a monthly basis, you must start doing that before teaching your children. Please do not allow them to leave your home and strike out on their own without knowing how to maintain a checkbook.

If you do not know how to balance your checkbook, then learn. Balancing your checkbook requires that you maintain a correct running balance in your check register. When you receive the bank statement, the amount *you* say you have must be reconciled to the amount the bank says you have.

The process of reconciliation involves (1) *adding* to *their* balance deposits you have made that have not yet been noted by the bank; (2) *subtracting* from *their* balance the checks that have not yet cleared the bank; then (3) *subtracting* from *your* balance any services or fees the bank has charged you which are not recorded in your check register. If the bank's balance and your balance do not agree, there is an error that needs to be found and corrected in your register or brought to the attention of the bank.

If you need specific instructions on how to balance your checkbook and reconcile it to the bank statement, ask your banker to explain how it is done. Most bankers are obliging and would be pleased to train you so that you, in turn, can train your children.

CREDIT CARDS

What is the best advice on credit cards? The problem is that we have, in the last fifteen years, become a credit card society, so much so that it is virtually impossible to operate financially without using credit cards. However, the truth of the matter is that credit cards violate almost every economic principle for personal money management.

The situation is similar to that of a man I read about in a Johannesburg, South Africa, newspaper many years ago. For some strange reason, a South African man wanted to set a record for living in a glass-enclosed cage with numerous black mamba snakes and cobra snakes, two of the most deadly snakes in the world. At the time I read the story, he had been in the cage for over thirty days living, eating, and sleeping among those snakes, any one of which could have killed him. He did not have any choice, once he had made the decision to be locked in the cage, other than to coexist with them. Yet I can guarantee you that none of those snakes became a friend to him. I feel similarly about our credit card society. It is exceedingly dangerous, yet it is absolutely essential that we learn to live with it! It is a fact of life. So, how do we live with it?

Credit cards violate almost every economic principle for personal money management.

People tell me all the time that credit cards are no problem to them because they use them only for convenience and pay off the outstanding balances every month. I certainly commend this practice, but I recognize that every time credit card companies put a credit card in someone's hands, they stimulate additional buying. For the most part, people buy articles they don't need, as I observed earlier.

Numerous studies by credit card companies have proved that spending by consumers will increase as much as 34 percent over what they would have spent if they had used cash. Many malls and stores have added their own credit cards to the nationally promoted credit cards, and they have found that consumer spending goes up. One credit card is not a replacement for other credit card spending; it is an addition.

In March 1986, *Forbes* magazine noted that "Americans carry 720,000,000 credit cards and the plastic is still proliferating. . . . At one mall in Newport Beach, California, sales grew nearly 10% in the first 10 months the new credit card was used." If these numbers were correct, there were roughly three credit cards outstanding for every man, woman, and child in the United States. If our family is average in terms of the number of credit cards, we should have three times seven, or twenty-one, different credit cards in our possession. Fortunately, that is not the case. Some other family must have our share of those cards. And consider what the average number would be now?

Credit card debt is the most expensive type of debt, generally costing between 18 and 21 percent of the outstanding credit card balance. Additionally, between 20 and 25 percent of a family's disposable income now goes to the payment of all consumer debt, which is credit card debt plus installment debt. Therefore, if a Christian family tithes 10 percent, pays taxes of approximately 15 percent of gross income, and has the normal consumer debt of 25 percent of disposable income, only 50 percent of the dollars coming into the household are available to meet any type of savings goal and the family living expenses. In the accounting profession we used to say, "Those numbers don't foot." In other words, they don't add up. A family cannot exist under those circumstances. However, families continue to add to their consumer debt to fund current consumption needs.

More and more Americans fall into the trap of credit card debt because advertisers aim deceptive and misleading advertising at them. To quote from a recent advertisement in a magazine, "Chase MasterCard—so far ahead in value, it actually pays to use it." In *Newsweek* magazine, October 28, 1985, an article entitled "A Green Giant Is on the Move" disclosed that American Express "will spend almost $500 million on marketing." And according to Howard Schneider, manager of Fee Services Marketing, "Our goal is to tie people to the card so they can't live without it."

You get the picture. The use of credit cards is a tremendous financial trap to fall into. They are deceptive, and the advertising dollars spent to get us to fall into the trap are in the billions. We really do believe spokespersons for American Express when they say "don't leave home without it."

There are two points to remember in training your children to use credit cards. First, if you use credit cards, use them wisely. Your children will model your behavior without question. Second, teach them how to use credit cards.

We believe that at some point while your children are still at home, they should be allowed to have a card and learn how to use it. But instead of the normal *credit* card, use a bank *debit* card. With this type of card an amount is deducted from the bank account when the card purchase is made. In other words, the card is used not as a financing tool, but as a convenience tool. Additionally, the debit card should not be used by either parents or children until they have, for at least one year and preferably two to three years, lived on a cash-only budget to establish the disciplines of planning and spending.

My counsel to parents who use credit cards is to take them, place them on a cookie sheet, preheat your oven to 450 degrees, and place the cookie sheet in the oven for fifteen minutes, or until all the cards melt. You will have a very pretty, multicolored piece of plastic. Second, live on cash only for one to two years. And if it will ease your mind, I will promise you that without even asking for them, all those credit cards can be replaced within two years. The credit card companies want you to use them. They love for you to pay them interest.

CARS

A primary area of conflict in families concerns cars. Parents should address the issue of cars and car expenses before it becomes an issue with the children. The decisions need to be made in advance and communicated to children so that they have plenty of time to understand and plan for them.

In my book, *Master Your Money*, I pointed out that the cheapest car you will ever own is the car you are presently driving. This is without exception unless the car is costing more in inconvenience than it is worth or unless the car becomes unsafe. Contrary to advertising and popular thought, no car is an investment. Only antique cars appreciate in value. Some cars hold their value more than others, but depreciation is the norm, not the exception. A person would be pretty foolish to buy an investment that was guaranteed not to appreciate. Therefore, how you view a car is going to affect the decisions you make regarding cars for you and for your children.

A question we ask ourselves regarding a car for our children is this: For whose convenience is the car? If the car is for our convenience, we choose the car, and we pay the expenses. For example, living in Atlanta, Georgia, it takes thirty minutes to get almost anyplace because of the traffic and the size of the city. We have felt that a car for our teenagers was essential just to reduce our own driving time. So we have purchased used—or, as our children would say, ancient—cars for each daughter when she reached age sixteen. They have used those cars for our convenience, not theirs. If they had wanted a different car, or if it were for their convenience, the decision would have been different. They would be able to choose whatever car they wanted, but they would pay for it and all its expenses. Very simply, it is either their choice or our choice.

◾ —————————————————————————————— ◾

The real purpose of a car is transportation, not "show" or "style."

◾ —————————————————————————————— ◾

We want them to understand two things. First, the real purpose of a car is transportation, not "show" or "style." Second, they need to know how much it would cost if they chose to drive a car for appearance' sake as well as for transportation purposes.

The issue of cars, and the expenses associated with them, should not be decided based on what parents can afford. Rather, it should have something to do with the degree of responsibility shown by children. It is amazing how many parents fall into the trap of feeling an obligation to provide for their children what their children desire to have. The parents forget the purpose of the car. Is it for the convenience of the parents or the children? That really is the determining factor as to who pays. However, children should be totally responsible for any fines and tickets they get, no matter who has purchased the car. They should also be required to pay the incremental insurance costs that come from driving irresponsibly.

◾ —————————————————————————————— ◾

Never have a car payment.

◾ —————————————————————————————— ◾

We have required our girls to provide a portion of the gas expenses because they are using the car some percentage of the time for their own needs and purposes. If they want to drive fifty miles on the weekend for entertainment purposes, that's fine as long as they pay for the gas to do so.

After they graduate from college, it is our objective to give them one-time help on buying a nice car, assuming that we can afford it at the time. That way they can begin their working life without having to make car payments.

I recently counseled with a young couple, one of whose father has "given them" a car upon graduation from college. The problem was that they were paying $450 a month in car payments and, therefore, were unable to make ends meet. When I questioned them, it turned out the father had made the down payment and set up the note for them to repay. As far as they were concerned, he had given them the car because it is the "standard way" to buy a car—on time. I thought to myself, *What a terrible gift that father has given.* They were deceived into thinking that they had a new car at no cost when, in fact, he had established for them the standard of car payments.

My counsel is simply this: Never have a car payment. Always pay cash for a car. Most people protest that they can't afford what they want if they do that. But I believe that you can't afford to drive it if you can't afford to pay cash. How do you get the cash to pay for that car? The old-fashioned way—save for it!

A COLLEGE EDUCATION

According to Ann Sturtevant, director of financial aid at Emory University and former regional director for Financial Aid Services for the College Board (*Atlanta Journal*, July 19, 1987),

People are usually willing to pay for something they value, yet parents find themselves balancing the benefits of a 4-year college education, which will cost about $27,000 at a typical public school, or more than $50,000 at a private school, with other family choices and priorities.

She adds,

> If parents are to overcome this "affordability crisis" they must first recognize that buying a college education constitutes one of the largest purchases they will ever make. Like any other major investment, financing college requires a planned, systematic approach and a combination of all the family's resources over a period of many years.

There are many ways to provide for a college education for your children. The least expensive is to require them to pay for it totally themselves, and the most expensive, of course, is to pay for it totally yourself.

The problem with paying for a college education is that it is paid with after-tax and after-tithe dollars. So if a four-year college education costs $27,000 at a public school, the parents must earn approximately twice that amount to have the $27,000 left to provide for the college costs. To make it very simple, if you multiply the number of children you have times $50,000, that is what you will have to earn to pay your taxes, tithe on your earnings, and still have enough left to send your children to a public college or university. You can double that amount if they go to a private university.

■ ──────────────────────────────── ■

There are many ways to provide for a college education for your children.

■ ──────────────────────────────── ■

How you fund college education is limited to basically four alternatives: (1) take money out of your current earnings, (2) save and invest ahead of time through one of many types of investment vehicles, (3) acquire student loans, (4) receive a scholarship, (5) require the student to work, or (6) a combination of all of the above. It is interesting to note that many parents who are sending their oldest children to college may not have paid off their own college loans yet.

■ ────────────────────────────── ■

Too often we parents become convinced that if we don't give our children what they want or think they want, they won't respect us or love us as much.

■ ────────────────────────────── ■

There is not a "right" or a biblical answer for how to fund college education. The most sensible way seems to begin saving early for college education costs so that when the children reach college age, the money is already there. Obviously, if you are going to do this, you will have to give up your own consumptive spending or earn a very, very large income. Whatever your decision as to how to fund college education, it is imperative that you make the decision early and communicate it clearly to your children so that they labor under no false expectations.

One young man from a fairly well-to-do family told me that he was going to pay for his college education because his father had paid for his own way through school. This had been communicated to the son the whole time he was growing up. He had absolutely no resentment about having to pay his way through school; in fact, he felt a sense of pride in meeting the challenge. I believe he had no resentment because his expectation all along was that he would pay for his college education. He obviously had great respect and admiration for his parents.

Too often we parents become convinced that if we don't give our children what they want or think they want, they won't respect us or love us as much. Quite the contrary is true. In reality we are trying to "buy" their acceptance of us. This feeling pervades our culture today.

If you are going to pay for your children's education, I have two suggestions. First, do not allow them to go to a school that you can't afford. In other words, *don't* borrow for college education costs. Second, give them the opportunity to manage money by giving them a lump sum for their college expenses. Let them manage the money throughout the year instead of sending them money on a weekly or a monthly basis. This is not to say that you can't send them some spending money periodically, but for the most part they should be able to manage a larger sum of money by the time they reach college age.

MAJOR PURCHASES

We have already discussed the major purchases like bicycles and cars. And we have looked at a major problem facing young marrieds today; that is, they expect to start where their parents left off, even though it may have taken their parents twenty-five years to get to that point.

One of the decisions that may confront you is whether or not to help your children purchase a home. We believe that it is important for children to be raised with the expectation that a home is not a "right." It is something that is earned.

Buying a home may not even be a wise financial decision. The accepted thinking has been that a home is the best investment people can make, and for the last forty years, that has probably been true. However, two basic assumptions underlie that thinking process: (1) inflation will continue to push the price of the home up, and (2) a fixed interest rate on the home mortgage loan will be available. As most people are well aware, appreciation in home values over the last few years has not been guaranteed in all sections of the country, and we saw home mortgage rates it the early 1980s climb to record levels.

Implicit in the decision to purchase a home using debt are the assumptions that there will be appreciation and that you can get a fixed interest rate. Before you make that purchase, you need to determine whether these assumptions are realistic.

Buying a home may not even be a wise financial decision.

I believe that if parents have the financial resources to do so, helping their children get into a home can give them a significant step toward accumulating some financial security. However, there are two big *ifs* in that assumption: if the parents can afford to, and if the parents desire to help in that way.

EMERGENCIES

We have made the decision to always be available to help our children meet emergency needs if, in fact, they have a real need, whether in college or after college while raising a family. Emergency needs could include medical problems, a handicapped child, loss of job, or other unplanned-for events.

Whether to meet the emergency with a loan or a gift is a very serious issue with potentially serious consequences. Proverbs 22:7 says, "The rich rules over the poor, / And the borrower is servant to the lender." Without question, when you lend money to anyone, be it a child, a friend, or a stranger, the borrower has become a servant to the lender. The relationship between the borrower and the lender becomes one of master–servant, regardless of the previous family relationship.

> *You cannot lend money or borrow money without getting into a master–servant relationship.*

You cannot lend money or borrow money without getting into a master–servant relationship. Consequently, I advise you to give the money rather than loan it when there is a *real* need by friends or children. If they choose to pay you back at a later date, that is fine. But do not set it up as a loan and create a barrier in your relationship.

Additionally, I would never loan money to children to satisfy their greeds. Where emergency needs end and greeds begin is a matter of judgment on the part of parents. I believe I would doubly violate biblical principles: I would change our relationship, and I would be encouraging ungodly behavior.

How to determine what is a greed and what is a need is not always easy. Basically, greeds are an indulgence of selfish desires and wants, whereas needs are the basics required for functioning in a given situation. For example, snow boots in upper Wisconsin are a need; a baseball uniform, if the child is on a baseball team, can be a need; textbooks for college are a need. On the other hand, a young married couple who want the money to buy a four-bedroom home or a new sports car is most likely satisfying a greed. They need housing or transportation, but wanting housing or transportation at a level that required the parents twenty years to attain is greed.

◼ —————————————————————————————— ◼

You must make your decisions very early and communicate them clearly.

◼ —————————————————————————————— ◼

CONCLUSION

Basically, you want expectation and reality to be in agreement for your children. If their expectation is something different from the reality of the situation, you will have conflict. If your children expect a brand-new car on their sixteenth birthday when you have no desire, plan, or willingness to give it to them, they will be disappointed, at the very least, and very possibly angry and resentful.

To harmonize their expectations and reality, you must make your decisions very early and communicate them clearly. Chart 14.1, Decision-Making Chart, will guide you into making some possible decisions. Then it is your responsibility to communicate them to your children. When you do this, reality and expectations will not be different, and a conflict is less likely to occur.

Be flexible. Be willing to be taught by your children and, most importantly, by our Lord. Listen and learn from them and Him.

CHART 14.1
DECISION-MAKING CHART
PARENTS' SUPPORT (ALLOWANCES) PER MONTH
(OR PER YEAR OR ONE TIME)

CATEGORIES	AGE			
	Preteen	Teen	College	Married
Budget				
Tithe	$_____	$_____	$_____	$_____
Save	$_____	$_____	$_____	$_____
Gift	$_____	$_____	$_____	$_____
Clothes	$_____	$_____	$_____	$_____
Spend	$_____	$_____	$_____	$_____
Total	$_____	$_____	$_____	$_____
Cars				
Purchase	N/A	$_____	$_____	$_____
Insurance	N/A	$_____	$_____	$_____
Gas, Oil, Maintenance	N/A	$_____	$_____	$_____
Repairs	N/A	$_____	$_____	$_____
Tires	N/A	$_____	$_____	$_____
College				
Tuition	N/A	N/A	$_____	$_____
Board/Room	N/A	N/A	$_____	$_____
Books	N/A	N/A	$_____	$_____
Emergencies	$_____	$_____	$_____	$_____
Major purchases	$_____	$_____	$_____	$_____
Loans	$_____	$_____	$_____	$_____

Leaving Wealth
To Children

T he cover of *Fortune* magazine on September 29, 1986, bore this question: SHOULD YOU LEAVE IT ALL TO THE CHILDREN? Inside, the article's lead paragraph was this:

Warren Buffett, 56, the Chairman and guiding genius of Berkshire Hathaway, the phenomenal successful holding company, is worth at least $1.5 billion. But don't bother being jealous of his three children. Buffett does not believe that it is wise to bequeath great wealth and plans to give most of his money to his charitable foundation. Having put his two sons and a daughter through college, the Omaha investor contents himself with giving them several thousand dollars each at Christmas. Beyond that, says daughter, Susan, 33, if I write my dad a check for $20, he cashes it.

With life insurance it is possible to leave substantial wealth to children when both parents have died. It may not be $1.5 billion, but it could be tens of thousands and perhaps several hundred thousand dollars. There is one major problem and several principles regarding estate planning that we will cover briefly in this chapter.

THE NEED FOR A WILL

The primary problem regarding estate planning is that more than 50 percent of Americans do not have a will. Consequently, it is a moot point when it comes to planning how wealth will be distributed. If there is no will, in many states, the surviving spouse has no say in the matter. It becomes the responsibility and function of the court system.

Many people suffer under the delusion that if they have a small estate, everything will go to the surviving spouse. Therefore, they see no reason to have a will. On the contrary, it may not all go to the spouse; it may be allocated among the children and the spouse. The spouse may not have much say over how the children's portion is managed, either. Additionally, without a will, if both parents should die in a common accident, the court will determine the guardian(s) of the children.

There are five good reasons to have a will other than being able to decide how wealth is to be distributed. First, with young children, the guardianship issue is determined. Second, personal possessions cannot be transferred according to your desires unless the will so states. Third, if you are a Christian, it is possible to put your testimony into your will so that the survivors and future generations will never have any question about your personal relationship with Jesus Christ. Fourth, if you desire to do any charitable giving at all at death, a will is absolutely the only way that this can be done. Fifth, if your estate is large enough that there is a potential estate tax problem, a will is the only way that estate tax planning can be done.

PRINCIPLES OF ESTATE PLANNING

The first principle of estate planning is that *it is dynamic.* Many people do not think about the fact that an estate plan is never operational until death; therefore, decisions that are made now can (and probably should) be changed as circumstances change. The number of children may change; their ages certainly will change. Physical handicaps of children or grandchildren and marriage partners of children are a consideration when it comes to estate planning. As circumstances change and facts become known, the estate plan can be changed through either codicils to a will or a revised will; both are very simple to do in terms of their execution. The difficult part comes in knowing what decisions to make.

■ ──────────────────────────────── ■

An estate plan is never operational until death ... decisions that are made now can (and probably should) be changed as circumstances change.

■ ──────────────────────────────── ■

The second principle is that you should never leave your children wealth unless you *leave them wisdom along with wealth.* Ecclesiastes 7:11–12 says,

> Wisdom is good with an inheritance,
> And profitable to those who see the sun.
> For wisdom is a defense as money is a defense,
> But the excellence of knowledge is
>   that wisdom gives life to those
>   who have it.

We are stewards of God's resources, and our last stewardship decision is to transfer God's resources to those who will handle them in accordance with His wishes. If one child has rebelled or is not walking in accordance with what God would have him to do, the last stewardship decision must be not to leave him any of God's resources.

To say it another way, you need to be willing to treat your children differently, and the only way you can do that it to remember whose resources you are passing on. Not only is godliness a consideration, but also their needs may differ. Certainly you would make different provisions if one were raising a handicapped child with inadequate resources and another was a single, highly successful professional or executive. Again, you are using God's resources to accomplish God's purposes, and I see nothing in Scripture that says your children must be treated on an equal basis.

You need to be willing to treat your children differently.

As with every other significant financial decision that we have discussed, expectations and reality must be in agreement; therefore, the third principle is that you should *communicate your desires and your estate plan* to your children. We have conducted many family conferences for our clients so that the parents have an opportunity to tell children what their desires are. We also share with the children how our clients have planned for their estate to be distributed. In almost every case, this has been done long before death.

The fourth principle is to *test and train your children through gifts of money* prior to leaving them a large estate. Here I am talking primarily to older people who have children in their thirties or forties. My advice is to give them large sums of money—be it five thousand dollars or fifty thousand dollars—to see how they handle the resources. You should expect them to make mistakes, but the important thing is what they learn by those mistakes. If you attach any strings to this kind of gift, however, it is no longer a gift. It is a bribe or a manipulative tool.

CONCLUSION

The key question you try to answer before leaving them wealth is this: What will that wealth do to them? If you find that it will cause them to fall from the faith or hinder their walk with the Lord, it would certainly be a poor decision to pass on that wealth to them. There are no right or wrong answers in this situation; only wisdom from above will allow you to make the right decision.

Here's My Problem

Through the years we have explained our teaching of money management issues to many couples. Often we will discuss with them a particular problem which their family is having trouble solving. In this chapter some of these problems will be examined. We will give specific recommendations as to how we have, or would, handle that situation, as well as highlight any principles involved. Perhaps some of these experiences also occur in your family.

PROBLEM: CONSISTENTLY FORGETTING TO GIVE AN ALLOWANCE

Not long ago I asked a fourteen-year-old girl how her parents handled her allowance. She told me that she no longer received an allowance because her parents could never seem to remember to give it to her. She constantly had to ask for the allowance, so her parents, in frustration, decided to give her money "as she needs it."

This situation seems to be very common. Parents cannot seem to remember to give the allowance consistently. So they throw up their hands in defeat and merely give money as children ask for it.

Solution

There are several ways to overcome this problem. First, you might pick a specific day of the month to give the allowance and never vary from that, such as the day you pay your monthly bills or payday. You will be less likely to forget one of these regular occasions.

Another approach that we have found to be very workable is to give the allowance on the first day of the month. I write on my calendar on the last day of the month to get the cash at the bank for the allowances. It always happens on the first day of the month. Another "helper" might be a chart on your mirror or refrigerator or even a note written to yourself in your checkbook. Perhaps a "foolproof" way would be to give the children the responsibility and freedom to remind you on a set day of the month that the allowance is going to be due in one or two days.

■ ─────────────────────────────────── ■

It is as important to pay the allowance on a regular basis as it is to make the mortgage payment.

■ ─────────────────────────────────── ■

Principles

Two underlying principles are important in overcoming this problem. First, habits take time to develop, and giving the allowance must become a habit. Therefore, you have to help yourself establish the habit. Second, giving the allowance should be as important to you as any other financial transaction. Because of what you are attempting to teach your children, it is as important to pay the allowance on a regular basis as it is to make the mortgage payment. The only difference is that your children are not likely to foreclose on you if you fail to give them their money.

PROBLEM: THE "SPENDER" CHILD

Invariably, people ask how to handle the child who wastes his money. He never seems to have any money left, and he puts pressure on the parents to give him extra money between the allowance payments.

Solution

The envelope system is probably the most effective way to cope with the spender child. The envelope system makes a child responsible for his own behavior; therefore, if he is frivolous with his money, he alone will bear the consequences of his actions. The great temptation for parents is to give more money when they know that the child has no more money, usually to avoid conflict for not doing so.

Principle

As we have stated in so many ways throughout the book, you have to give children the freedom to fail, and you must allow them to bear the consequences of their own decisions. It is most difficult with a spender child because you know that he is failing so often.

PROBLEM: THE "HOARDER" CHILD

How do you handle the child who won't spend her money? Once a couple told me that when one daughter was younger, they would give her money for refreshments before they went somewhere—to the county fair, for example. However, the daughter would not spend the money for something to drink, even though she was thirsty. Instead she would ask her mother to buy her something to drink. Once the "hoarder's" dollar bill was broken, however, she had no problem in spending the rest.

Another example is the child who will not spend money on clothes that are needed. In other words, the money itself has a much higher priority than peer pressure or parental pressure.

We are sure that many parents would like to have this problem because most children are just the opposite. It is a real problem, however, if the money is not being spent as it was intended. Presumably the money was given in the first place on the basis of anticipated need.

Solution

Dealing with a child who has the problem of hoarding may be best solved by using what we would call *the government approach*. In setting its budgets for the various departments and agencies on a year-to-year basis, the government will reduce the following year's budget by any amount left unspent at the end of the current year. As a consequence, of course, the agencies and departments are motivated to spend everything in the budget before the end of the year.

This technique will undoubtedly work with a child by merely reducing the amount she will get in the next month, or year, by any amounts left. In order to ensure that she does not "cheat" on the system, you may have to require an accounting of where the money has been spent however.

Principles

Try to determine why the child won't spend. Probably, the problem is not money. It may very well be a security problem, or even a sin problem, in the sense of selfishly hoarding.

The classic story in the Bible dealing with this is that of the rich young fool who built barns and hoarded grain to no avail (see Luke 12:16–21). His perspective was entirely short-term, and he forgot that we are given resources for the purpose of using them.

Money, of course, is always a resource and not an end in itself. Money is to be used—not spent; it should be viewed as a resource, used to accomplish some end. On the other hand, when money is considered merely something to be *spent*, it is often handled frivolously rather than wisely.

PROBLEM: CHILDREN'S FRIENDS GETTING FAR MORE MONEY THAN YOUR KIDS DO

This is a very common and difficult problem to handle. How do you handle the situation when you let your children go shopping with friends? Your children are on a set budget, but the friends show up at the shopping center with a handful of credit cards for whatever they want to buy. Not only that, but their parents have set no limit on what they can spend.

That may be an extreme example, but it certainly happens in our society today. Your problem may be one of the six-year-old down the street getting two dollars per week and your six-year-old getting one dollar per week.

Solution

The solution seems to involve a sequence of steps. First, gather your facts. Are your children telling you the whole story about friends' allowances? This may require making telephone calls to some parents or having your children verify the information. Second, be willing to reevaluate the budget amount that you are giving your children. Third, make your children part of the process of evaluation and reevaluation. And fourth, if you still feel that you are doing exactly as you should after gathering the facts and reevaluating the budget, be firm in your decision, and do not succumb to the pressure.

Principles

This is a problem each of us deals with every day of our lives. Except for the richest man or woman in the world (whoever that is), there will *always* be others with more money and/or less discipline. Succumbing to the pressure of what others do is *not* a money problem; it is a values and self-discipline problem. You, as a family, will have certain values that are reflected in the way you spend money; because someone else has "different" values does not make the "different" values right. That is why it is important to be firm in your decisions. Spending because others spend is never wise.

Solving this particular problem may be the greatest teaching opportunity you have. Don't overlook the opportunity by caving in to the pressure from your children.

■ —————————————————————————— ■

Succumbing to the pressures of what others do is not a money problem; it is a values and self-discipline problem.

■ —————————————————————————— ■

PROBLEM: GRANDPARENTS GIVING UNWARRANTED AND LARGE GIFTS TO CHILDREN

Many grandparents give their grandchildren cash and other gifts that the parents would not give, or could not afford to give, to their children. Many times grandparents give grandchildren *anything* they want. Grandparents may also treat each grandchild differently and unequally.

This interference often undermines the authority of the parents and destroys any success the parents might have in training their children to be financially responsible. Some grandparents feel that they have a "right" to spoil their grandchildren, that this is how grandparents are "supposed" to behave. You may even find yourself challenged if you interfere with this "right" in any way.

Solution

Our recommendation regarding this problem is to pick one or more of the following alternatives. The first and best alternative is to lovingly confront them with what they are doing. Do this after you have a teaching system, such as the envelope system, in place so that the *system* becomes the standard—not you, and certainly not them. Perhaps you can even ask them to participate with you in the system. By doing so you may be able to point out the behavior that is giving you a problem.

A second idea is to present them with an alternative to the large gift. For example, you could ask them to set up savings accounts for your children instead of giving gifts. Or you could ask them to put the money in a college fund. You could also ask them to spend time, rather than money, with your children, which probably is of more value to the children than money. A relationship with their grandparents is a blessing they can never purchase. The grandparents could choose to give gifts, but you should have a *limit* on the *amount* of the gifts. That way you will not take the pleasure away that they get out of giving, and they will not thwart what you want to teach.

Third, your children could accept financial gifts but put them in their savings accounts. Then at some point they can share with their grandparent how they used the total of the gifts given to them.

A last alternative is to teach your children to say, "No, thank you," to their grandparents. There is obviously great risk in choosing this alternative in terms of the relationship with the grandparents, but you may have no other alternative. This method is to be used only when you have tried everything else and your children's well-being is at stake. You have to be careful, though, not to put your children in an adversarial relationship with their grandparents. It is not the children's fault.

Principles

Unfortunately, there is not an easy solution to this problem. It will most likely come down to what is most important to you—your children's well-being, your relationship with the grandparents, or the principle involved. If the children's well-being is involved, it may be worth risking the relationship in order to ensure the children's development. The relationship with the grandparents is certainly one to be treasured and cultivated. However, when it stands in the way of teaching your children the principles of living a successful and godly life, you may need to stand firm and risk the relationship. If it is a matter of principle, you must decide if you want to risk the relationship for the principle.

PROBLEM: WANTING YOUR CHILDREN TO DO AS YOU *SAY*—NOT AS YOU *DO*

This problem comes to us typically stated as follows: "There are many things I *do*, or *don't do*, that I don't want them to learn. I don't tithe; I don't save; I don't budget; I don't balance my checkbook; I do spend impulsively; and I do overuse my credit cards. How can I teach my children not to do these things when for years they have seen me make every mistake in the book?"

Solution

We have addressed this problem from several different angles throughout this book, but if we were going to summarize it, we would say that you need to do the following:

1. Confess your failures to your children.

2. Ask for their forgiveness.

3. Forgive yourself.

4. Read *Master Your Money* to get the basics of money management.

5. Change your behavior one step at time.

Principles

The first principle underlying this problem is forgiveness. God has forgiven us through Jesus Christ; and we, in turn, need to forgive others. So, you need to ask for forgiveness and be willing to forgive yourself.

The second principle is that God will do His part to change your behavior *if* you do your part. Your part consists of taking steps in obedience to His direction; His part is to provide the power to do so, as He has promised. God has given us His Holy Spirit to enable us to be *all* He calls us to be.

Your part can begin with a commitment to remember that God owns it all. Then you must make a commitment to exercise self-discipline and begin to develop a spending, saving, and tithing plan.

Our challenge to you is to determine what the first step should be, take the step, and watch God work in your life and in your children's lives. Don't try to hide your failures from your children; they know far more than you would really like for them to know. They are very wise in their observations and almost nothing can be hidden from them.

PROBLEM: A CHILD WITH
SPECIAL NEEDS

One of your children may be gifted in some way or may have an interest in a certain area, such as sports, ballet, or art. She might also require special education because of her talent or because of a learning or physical disability. Is it fair to treat this child differently from her brothers and sisters? If you give one child extra money for sports, for example, should her siblings get a similar amount to use as they would like?

Solution

The answer to this problem is simple, but implementing it may not be. The answer is that no child will ever be equal to brothers or sisters or anyone else in life. Therefore, children do not have to be treated equally. What is important is that you treat each of your children with justice and fairness and that you love them equally.

The way to deal with this particular problem is to prepare budget sheets for each of them individually, along with their help, and then handle them according to their needs. When they are a part of the process of setting the budgets and standards, they are more likely to be convinced that the system is fair and that they are not being mistreated.

Principle

The Scripture is clear that we are all uniquely created, even twins, as for example, Jacob and Esau. Even though the biblical patriarchs had large families, they did not treat all their children the same. See Jeremiah 1:5, Psalm 119:73, Isaiah 43:7, and Isaiah 44:24.

PROBLEM: HANDLING THE "SPENDER" ALONG WITH THE GOOD MONEY MANAGER

Children are naturally going to be different from one another. We have a family of five, and we see five different personalities. Consequently, they have five different ways of viewing and managing money. It is not a matter of the age or sex of the children.

Solution

The envelope system frees you to train them as unique individuals. The system becomes the standard and the tool and helps you to communicate that you are on their team, making the system work.

Principle

Realize that individual views are not right or wrong. Recognize that each child is unique and that money is a tool to be used by God to accomplish character development. Good stewardship is the goal in training your children—not that they spend their money the same way.

PROBLEM: ONE CHILD TAKING FINANCIAL ADVANTAGE OF A SIBLING

What do you do with a child who sells toys or clothing to a younger brother or sister at an exorbitant price? Or what about the child who has the ability to con his sibling out of what he wants at far too cheap a price? Included in this problem is the child who borrows from his siblings and never repays them. From our experience, it seems that every family with more than one child will have to face this problem at some time or another.

Solution

We always reserve the right to be arbitrators in these situations, with our word being the final word. We believe that after the first time, there should be a penalty for further unfair transactions. The penalty probably should be a monetary one. For example, if a child buys his brother's new baseball, which cost four dollars, for fifty cents, we would consider requiring that the purchaser pay the full fair value of four dollars plus a two dollar penalty. He would not have the option of returning the baseball.

Principles

It is important to deal with this behavior because the one who is allowed to win unjustly may develop an attitude problem. The book of Proverbs says that the Lord hates a false balance. The principle here is that dealing unfairly with others is causing the offender to be "hated" by the Lord. The world has paraphrased this to say that "cheaters never win and winners never cheat." In other words, be fair with one another. The behavior needs to be dealt with severely because it is the *behavior*, not the child, that is wrong. God loves the sinner but hates the sin.

> *There is a price to be paid for leniency*
> *and lack of self-discipline on our part;*
> *that price will be paid for over*
> *many generations.*

PROBLEM: GIVING THEM MONEY WHEN THEY ASK, EVEN THOUGH THEY HAVE ALREADY RECEIVED THEIR ALLOWANCE

A friend shared with us that when he and his sister were growing up, their parents gave them whatever they wanted. He was a good money manager, but his sister was not. His sister married a man who cannot afford to give her whatever she wants, and they have had tremendous difficulties in their marriage because she had learned to equate love with being able to have whatever she wanted.

We need to know that there is a price to be paid for leniency and lack of self-discipline on our part; that price will be paid for over many generations.

Solution

The solution to the problem is to ask yourself, Why do I continually give in to my children? Is it an attempt to buy their love and loyalty? Is it because we feel guilty? Or is it because of the attitude that my children should not have to experience the hard times I did?

What you are teaching them by being so lenient. You are probably teaching them that there are no limits or that it is possible to buy love. You may even be improving their manipulation skills by allowing them to talk you into buying whatever they want.

The way to deal with the problem is to determine if they are running short because of an inadequate budget. If the answer to that is no, when you give them extra money, have them pay you back out of their next allowance. If you "loan" them money when you are away from home, be sure they pay you back when you get home. This is difficult to do with children because you tend to feel guilty when they pay you back small amounts, but you must remember what *not* having them pay you back can cause in terms of their expectations.

It is okay for you to have the freedom to give spontaneously, as long as that is not the expectation of the children. A couple heard our description of the training system, and they implemented it with their four children. A few weeks later they were out shopping at a mall, and the mother suggested that they all get a cookie. The youngest child broke into tears. When he was asked why, he replied, "I don't want to spend my money on a cookie." The mother wisely said, "No, honey, you don't understand. *This is my treat.*" She said that, and the children's eyes lighted up as she purchased the cookies.

The mother felt that the children had learned that the cookie really was a treat. Had they not been using the money management system, they would not have appreciated it as much. How many of us have thought about what it takes to make our children grateful?

Another friend of ours said it this way, "Until there is a limit, there is no value to money." He also shared with us that until they had set up a budget for their children, they did not realize how much they were actually giving them—a dollar or five dollars at a time.

Principle

There is a limited supply of money. Children—and adults do well to learn this truth.

PROBLEM: THE CHILD WHO PLAYS ONE SPOUSE AGAINST THE OTHER

It is not at all uncommon for one spouse to be committed and the other uncommitted to the training process. It occurs many times when parents are divorced, but that is not always the case. Many married couples do not have unity when it comes to training their children.

This problem occurs when a child actively and knowingly plays one parent against the other. For example, in the case of divorced parents, a child may threaten to move out and live with the other parent if he doesn't get *his* way in money matters. This, of course, is not a money problem; money is just being used as the lever. The real problem is one of discipline.

Solution

The solution to this problem is similar to the one for the problem of overindulgent grandparents. First, and best of all, the offender should be confronted. You can hope that when confronted, the child will change behavior. If, however, he will not change, our advice to you is twofold: don't play "the game" and get caught in the trap; and don't take the conflict out on the child.

Principles

Basically, this whole problem becomes a faith issue. If you are doing your part by being a role model and training the child to manage money, you have fulfilled your responsibility. Even though you may not see the results in the child in the short term, in the longer term we all know that God is faithful, and He is able to deal with the offending parent and the child. It will not be easy, but we believe that the matter is well worth the commitment and faith required.

PROBLEM: THE CARELESS CHILD

Parents typically describe this problem by saying, "Our child continually loses books, jackets, and sweaters (really basic things), and we are frequently having to replace them out of our money. If we don't she may get cold, do poorly in school, or suffer in other ways."

Don't take on a responsibility that is the child's.

Solution

Our advice is very simply this: Don't take on a responsibility that is the child's. In other words, don't feel obligated to replace what he or she lost out of your money. If you feel you have to replace whatever it is, at least require the child to pay for it out of the next month's allowance or require him or her to earn the money to pay for it.

You may want to consider an escalating penalty. For example, the first time she forgets her purse, you will help her find it or replace it. The second time, she will have to replace it *and* compensate you for the time taken in looking for the purse. The third time, you may make also her pay you a taxi rate to drive her back to look for it.

These recommendations may sound harsh to you. You may prefer to use the loss-of-reward method that we described in an earlier chapter. You could give ten dollars in quarters or an envelope of one-dollar bills on the first of the month. Every time she loses her purse or sweater or something, she loses a dollar or a quarter of the envelope or jar. She can then keep whatever is left over at the end of the month. We have found this to be very effective in establishing habits.

Principles

The principle is that we are all responsible for our own actions, and we must bear the consequences of those actions. If parents continually step in and remove any consequences for actions, the child never has a hope of learning this most important principle.

PROBLEM: GIVING TO YOUR CHILDREN OUT OF A SENSE OF GUILT

Many parents give to their children out of a sense of guilt for a divorce, a drinking problem, too much travel, or some important "commitment" that keeps them from being with the children. In essence, they are attempting to "pay" for the lack of time or attention.

You cannot buy love or pay for a wrong suffered. When you give in to them financially, you are compounding the problem because your problem becomes their problem expressed in a different way.

Solution

This book does not offer professional psychological advice. If you believe that you are dealing with a sense of guilt, you should seek help in Christian counseling. The symptom may be a financial problem, but the root cause is far more complex than the symptom. This must be solved for your sake and for the children's sake.

PROBLEM: CHARGE YOUR CHILDREN FOR THE USE OF YOUR POSSESSIONS

One of our friend's son wanted to set up a lawn-mowing business and to use his dad's lawn mower in this business. The father decided to charge his son for using his tools in this way.

Solution

It is a good idea to charge a child for the use of your possessions when they are producing income. You can teach them the true cost of doing business.

An alternative to charging them is to go into partnership with them and, in return for your contribution of the tools and expertise, participate in the profits of the enterprise. Another one of my good friends also has a son who started a lawn-mowing business when he was twelve years old, financed by his father. The son paid the loans back, and by the time he graduated from high school, he had saved $10,000 in the bank and had purchased almost $30,000 worth of equipment. He was able to sell his business and the equipment and fund his way through college. This young man has learned financial responsibility.

Principle

There is a cost to having the resources necessary to conduct a business.

PROBLEM: LOANING MONEY TO YOUR CHILDREN

Even though our advice earlier in the book was never to loan money to children, we were primarily referring to grown children. We believe there are some instances when it is okay to loan money to your children.

Solution

Loaning money to children can be an opportunity to teach them. If you loan them money when they are younger, you can teach the cost of borrowing. We know of parents who have loaned their children money and charged them interest so that the children realize that borrowing money is not "free." It is better to learn this at a young age than later in life when the cost of the mistake can become severe.

Before loaning them money, you need to think about why they need the money. Is it because of poor planning? Do they have a habitual problem? Is it an emergency, or is it some opportunity they have? If it is the result of poor planning, we most likely would not lend money to them. On the other hand, an emergency and an unexpected opportunity are legitimate times to either give or loan money.

Principle

Again, what are you attempting to teach your children? Charging them interest at an early age may be a good way to teach them a very important lesson of life: There is no free lunch.

PROBLEM: A CHILD WHO IS GETTING READY TO MAKE A REALLY STUPID DECISION

Since children learn financial maturity at the cost of their mistakes, it is often difficult for parents to know just when to step in and forestall the consequences of their child's bad decision.

Solution

The real question is, How far do you go in allowing a child the freedom to fail? The answer depends on several things. First, how serious is the mistake going to be? For example, allowing a child to spend a dollar foolishly at the grocery store is far different from allowing him or her to purchase an unsafe automobile at age sixteen. One child may want to wear name brand shirts or jeans, whereas another places a higher value on a stereo system.

It also depends on the age of the child and where he is in the learning process. You are certainly going to want to give much more advice at an earlier age than you will later on.

"Stepping in" and "giving advice" are two different things. If you "step in," you stop him from making a mistake by forcing the issue and not allowing him to fail. "Advising" him before he makes the decision and then allowing him to choose is something entirely different. It is a judgment call as to when you step in and when you give advice; but examine the situation to see which is appropriate response. God will give you the wisdom to make the right decision.

We are very free with our advice to our children. We don't even necessarily wait to be asked, but we do let them know that we won't love them any less if they choose against our advice. We try to help them see beforehand that they will have to live with the choice they make. When they understand the long-term implications of a choice, and that our love is not dependent upon their choosing what we would choose, they experience freedom and security in their decision.

Principles

Again let us say that our children's choices on how to spend their money are often not the same as ours would be. However, *they are not wrong*—they are just different. They reflect each child's personality. Let each be free to express himself by his choices, assuming they are scripturally sound. Your child's confidence and self-respect will grow as he realizes he can to make decisions that are different from those you would make.

CONCLUSION

As parents, we're challenged and stretched, many times beyond our own limitations, through the process of raising our children. The encouraging part of this is that God is well able to provide the wisdom we need in the situations we face. Memorize and apply daily James 1:5 which states, "If any of you lacks wisdom, let him ask of God, who gives to all liberally and without reproach, and it will be given to him." We don't have all of the answers, but we know the Source who does. God is not only growing our children up, but He is growing us up as well. It is necessary for each of us to continually ask God what He would have us to learn.

Another verse that we feel is critical to application of these principles is Hebrews 11:6: "But without faith it is impossible to please Him, for he who comes to God must believe that He is, and that He is a rewarder of those who diligently seek Him." Training your children requires faith. "Faith comes," the Bible says, "not only by hearing the Word, but by doing it" (see James 2:17).

Remember as you begin the great adventure of training your children to manage their money that God will guard and keep what you have committed to Him (Eph. 3:20). Children are children, and mistakes tend to be the same from one generation to the next. God is far more able to meet our children's needs than we are and far more concerned about the training responsibility than we are. He will provide us with what we need, when we need it, to train up His children in His ways.

With that in mind, we'll leave you with one of our favorite passages found in Philippians 4:6–7: "Be anxious for nothing, but in everything by prayer and supplication, with thanksgiving, let your requests be made known to God; and the peace of God, which surpasses all understanding, will guard your hearts and minds through Christ Jesus."

Readers of *Raising Money-Smart Kids*
will also enjoy Ron Blue's *Master Your Money*

Will I ever have enough?
Will it continue to be enough?
How much *is* enough?

If you can't answer these questions, *Master Your Money* will!

In *Master Your Money*, popular financial counselor Ron Blue has combined the Bible's timeless teachings on stewardship and responsibility with the most modern insights on financial management and cash control. With detailed charts and worksheets and a handy glossary of money terms, *Master Your Money* is the money book you've been waiting for. You'll wonder why you weren't told these concepts years ago!

Here are some of the exciting strategies in Master Your Money:

- *The "3 percent rule" for beating inflation*
- *How to see past the "Four Great Money Myths"*
- *Ways to recognize a truly good deal on anything*
- *The magic of compounding*
- *How to determine your "Propensity to Borrow" ratio*
- *Tips on controlling your cash flow*
- *Six ways to get out of debt* now
- *How to set faith goals that support financial goals*

You *can* MASTER YOUR MONEY!

Master Your Money, available now at your
Christian bookstore

About the Authors

Ron Blue is the managing partner for Ronald Blue & Co., an Atlanta-based firm offering financial planning, investment management, and tax services to individual and corporate clients throughout the United States. Ron received his MBA degree from Indiana University. He is the author of *Master Your Money* and *The Debt Squeeze,* with more than 150,000 copies in print. He is also the developer and creator of two videos: "Master Your Money" and "Common Cents: Training Your Children to Manage Money." He frequently writes for various Christian publications and is a regular contributor to *Moody Monthly* and Focus on the Family's *Physician* Magazine.

Judy Blue is a graduate of Indiana University, with a bachelor's degree in speech and hearing therapy and a master's degree in counseling and guidance. Ron and Judy have been married for twenty-seven years and are the parents of five children, ages fourteen through twenty-five.